Floyd
UNCORKED

Floyd UNCORKED

⑤ THE BOOK OF THE HIT CHANNEL 5 SERIES

JONATHAN PEDLEY
WITH **KEITH FLOYD**

Harper
Collins
Illustrated

The TV series 'Floyd Uncorked' is executive produced and directed by Nick Patten.

Nick Patten Productions Ltd would like to thank Wendy J. Rollason, Niall Fraser, François Gandolfi, Mike Wood, Rick Lord, Alexandra Taylor, John Baldwin, Steve Butts of Edge & Ellison and Michael Attwell at Channel Five.

Keith Floyd is represented by Stan Green Management, Dartmouth, Devon.

Nick Patten Productions Ltd and HarperCollins*Publishers* wish to thank all those wine producers in France and their agents in Britain who so generously donated wine for photography.

First published in 1998 by HarperCollins*Publishers*. This paperback edition published in 1999 by HarperCollins*Publishers*

Text © Nick Patten Productions Ltd 1998
Photographs © HarperCollins*Publishers* 1998
Channel 5 logo © Channel 5 Broadcasting Limited 1998

A catalogue record for this book is available from the British Library.

ISBN 0 00 414098 2

Editor: Silvija Davidson
Indexer: Susan Bosanko
Cartographer: Martin Brown
Food photographs: Michelle Garrett
Home Economist: Joanna Farrow

Photographic Credits:
Pages 32, 36, 59, 64-5, 81, 96, 130: **Michael Busselle**, pages 90-91: **Chris Fairclough Colour Library,** pages 39, 64(top right), 68, 116: **Holt Studios**, pages 10-11, 13, 15, 30, 30-31, 38-9, 52-3, 54, 56, 64(top middle), 66, 67, 74-5, 74(top left & top middle), 76, 77, 90(top left & top right), 92(top middle), 93, 95, 99 101, 114, 124(top left), 124-5, 127: **Pix**
All other photographs: **Kim Sayer**
Bottle photographs: **Anthony Cambio**

Colour origination by Saxon Photolitho Ltd
Printed and bound in Italy by Rotolito Lombarda Spa

Keith Floyd was born in 1943 and educated at Wellington School, Somerset. Since then he has devoted his life to cooking, except for a few brief excursions into the army and the antiques and wine trades. He has presented 13 highly successful television cookery and travel series, recently including 'Floyd Uncorked', and is the author of 15 bestselling books, including *Floyd on Oz, Floyd on Spain, Far Flung Floyd, Floyd on Italy, Floyd on Hangovers, Floyd on Africa*, and *A Feast of Floyd*, which is published by HarperCollins. When he is not hurtling around the world, he spends his time fishing and sailing in Marbella, Spain, where he now lives.

Having studied Biochemistry at Oxford, it was apparent to Jonathan Pedley that neither he nor his subject were likely to benefit from further acquaintance. With a research career thus eliminated, what to do? The wine trade appeared to be a civilised and benign way to waste one's life, so Jonathan wrote his 50 'giz- a-job' letters and was taken on by Grants of St James's. He spent periods working in buying, sales, marketing and distribution before getting involved in re-establishing the School of Wine. In 1994 Jonathan was able to establish the School as a stand-alone organisation. Jonathan has also acted as wine consultant to Carlsberg-Tetley for the last four years. Recent projects include making a wine video with Keith Floyd, and lecturing at Edith Cowan University in Perth. Jonathan passed the gruelling Master of Wine course in 1992, joining an institute which still numbers just over two hundred members worldwide. He lives with his wife, Ruth, and daughter, Ellen, in London.

CONTENTS

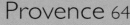

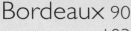

FOREWORD

Before I try to introduce this book, mostly written by my professorial wine-sniffing chum, Jonathan Pedley MW (that is to say, Master of Wine – or should that be educated alcoholic), who has dedicated his palate and intellect to unravelling the mysteries and pleasures of wine drinking, I should point out to you that as far as my own contribution is concerned – basically a few notes on a couple of classic provincial dishes and a few thoughts on a few wines, from a man who has devoted not so much his brain, but more his liver to eating and drinking the finer things in life – that the information I impart should be taken with a huge pinch of salt. For example, in my recipes, quantities, cooking times and temperatures are approximate. Equally, dates, times and vintages are quite likely to be inaccurate. This is not a text book. It is, from my point of view, a very personal, albeit brief, guide to some of the good things you can find in France.

First, let me state that I do not believe that we must drink white wine with fish or red wine with meat. I don't even believe we have to drink wine at all, if we don't like it. You must drink what you like, when you like and with what you like. That's the disclaimer over.

When I first went to France in about 1960 or 1961, pale blue Renault Dauphines, battleship-grey, long-nosed Peugeot 203 pickup trucks and black Citroën *tractions avants* à l'Inspector Maigret, little corrugated 2CV vans and Fourgonettes (which when they died were dumped in vineyards and fields and used as sheds) sped along the plane tree lined, narrow roads. At this time when the French Sou was made of aluminium and had a hole in the

middle, and when all you knew about French culture, food and wine was that they ate frogs' legs and snails and drank wine from five-starred plastic-stoppered litre bottles, I was hitch-hiking to a place called Blois, a small town on the River Loire. I was given a lift by a ferrety-faced man with an engorged red nose and purple veins that matched his sweat-soaked beret, who sucked on a thick, fat cigarette wrapped in yellow maize paper, called a *brouillard* (it was a *gitane* in any event) *papier mais*. It was getting dark on this long, straight road and he said I would get no further that night, but I was welcome to sleep in his house. At the time, I was unaware that he was drunk and probably had not been home for some days and was possibly using me as an excuse to explain his absence to his wife. During the short journey of 30 or 40 kilometres we stopped frequently to drink glasses of bitter, cheap wine. He hammered at the door of his decrepit house, which appeared to be a smallholding with a neat vegetable garden, a few ducks and chickens and a flatulent pig that lay in an untended flower bed. The house inside was dimly lit with an unshaded, low wattage light bulb and his wife was cooking something in a chipped blue enamel pot. He ordered his wife to feed me from the pot of white beans and sausage, ejected his young children, who shared a single bed smelling of urine, and let me sleep.

The following morning, after a murky cup of grainy, thick black coffee and half a loaf of crunchy bread, spread thick with unsalted butter and homemade apricot jam, I continued my journey to Blois to find myself in a small café overlooking the Loire, where workmen were breakfasting on white wine, and perch and dace only two or three inches long, about the size of sardines, cooked under a small, stainless steel, electric grill. That evening, for supper in what I suppose was a bed and breakfast, I faced the embarrassment of eating an artichoke filled with hollandaise sauce. I couldn't see how a knife and fork could work, in fact I didn't even know what an artichoke was, didn't know if I could afford the meal and didn't know what I had ordered, but a kindly lady told me how to remove the leaves of the artichoke and suck the flesh from the bottom. When a kind of potted pork paste arrived in a big earthenware terrine, was I to eat it all? Was that my main course? I took a little and tentatively tried the little gherkins that were placed on the dish beside it. I was then brought what I think was a piece of veal – I had never tasted veal – in what seemed to be a mustard-flavoured sauce. My limited French had enabled me to order 'un pichet de Vin de Pays'. They gave me a thin slice of glazed apple tart on a crisp, slightly burnt pastry base and, to my surprise, then brought a wicker basket of cheeses such as I had never seen before. Throwing caution to the winds, I ordered coffee and accepted something called a *digestif*, a fiery alcohol that tasted of raspberries. Later I was to discover *eau-de-vie de framboise*.

I spent a few aimless, lonely days wandering around and decided to head for home, hitch-hiking again. The first car to stop was a 1954 black Rolls Royce, towing a trailer with a Bugatti on it. They took me from Blois to Calais and at Dover we said goodbye and I hitched home, fired by a passion and a misunderstood love of France and French cooking. Hungry for knowledge and information, I stumbled by divine intervention on three books that changed my life: Elizabeth David's 'French Country Cooking', Len Deighton's classic strip-cartoon cookbook, 'Où est le Garlic?' and Gabriel Chevallier's classic

about a Burgundian village, 'Clochemerle'. But all of that was well over thirty years ago, since when the vicious tide of nouvelle cuisine has flooded and ebbed, we have travelled more and enjoyed the *tom yam gungs* of Thailand and the *arroz a banda* of Spain, become infatuated with the Pacific rim cooking of California and Australia, savoured the joys of *nems* from Vietnam, chicken *satays* from Malaysia, beef *rendang* from Indonesia, and *biryani* of rice and chicken from India; we have had *dim sum* in Hong Kong, *sushi* in Japan, *tabbouleh* from the Lebanon and *couscous* from Morocco; and yet, despite even American imperialistic colonisation of the gastronomic world via McDonalds and Kentucky Fried Chicken, France still remains in most people's hearts as the mother of all kitchens.

But as I explained at the outset, or at least I think I explained, whereas I have devoted my liver to one of the greatest *causes célèbres*, to wit, enjoying wine, I have never really bothered to turn my enjoyment into a science or an art, nor to worry about which grape makes which wine. I have been unconcerned about the attributes of a Merlot or a Sauvignon Blanc or a Pinot Noir, and that is why it has been such a pleasure to work with JP, who will explain the intricacies and the basic facts of the drink in your glass. Cheers!

Keith Floyd

Keith Floyd, Spain 1998

INTRODUCTION

Stay calm. This book is intended to be a low stress introduction to wine in general, and French wines in particular.

Despite the amount of wine we drink nowadays, the whole subject remains intimidating for many of us. The sheer volume of information which exists about wine is mind boggling even for people in the drinks business. Fortunately, to enjoy wine the only crucial knowledge you need is how to get a cork out of a bottle.

However, as with many things in life, we have a sneaking feeling that if we understand something just a little better, our appreciation of it will be that much deeper. The complexities of French wine are not something that can be tackled at one sitting. The best approach is gradually to build up an understanding of what is going on, with a generous allowance of the relevant wine imbibed as you go along. After all, you may die before you learn to recite all the Grands Crus of Burgundy in reverse alphabetical order (and you would no doubt deserve to be dead if you could). Each chapter of this book is devoted to one of the main vineyard regions in France. As well as describing the principal styles of wine produced in each region, we have included tasting notes on some of the benchmark examples. Also to be found in each chapter are chunks of technical information, covering general issues about how grapes are grown, how wine is made, and how to store and serve it correctly. In addition, Keith will be describing some of the classic foods of the region, and giving a recipe or two using local specialities. If you are a glutton for punishment and want to tackle the whole of the technical information on its own, in the Appendix at the back of the book I have suggested a reading order for the technical chunks. There is also a suggested list of further reading if you want to pursue the subject further.

There is a lot to learn about French wine. But by and large it is worth it. Many of France's classic wines remain the reference points for winemakers the world over. I always say to students on my wine courses that if they understand what is going on in France, then they are well over half way to understanding the rest of the world's wines.

Jonathan Pedley, London 1998

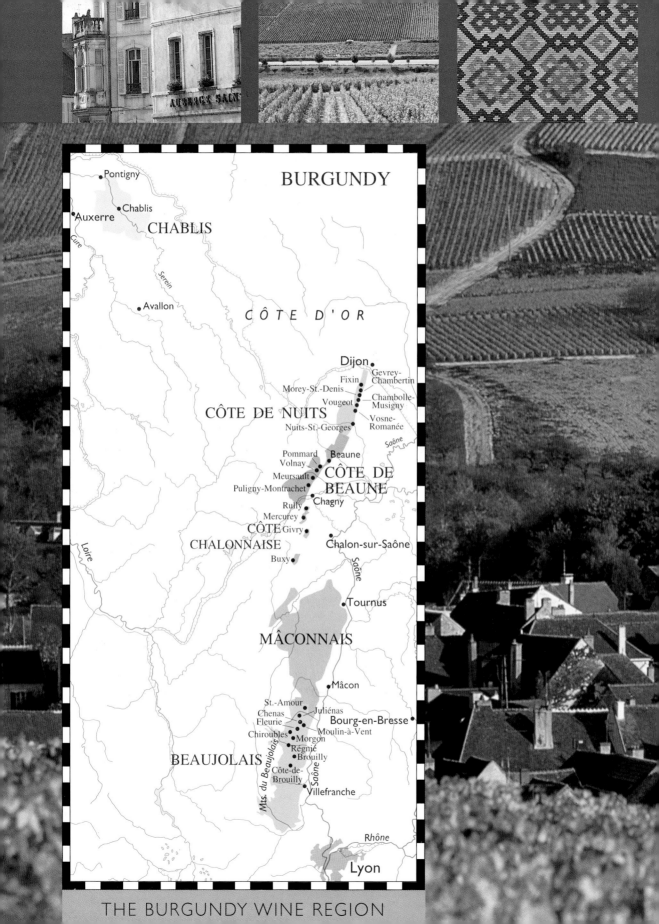

THE BURGUNDY WINE REGION

BURGUNDY

*I*t is appropriate that our journey around France should start in Burgundy. The wines of this region can be exceptional, as can the food, and allied with the cultural richness make Burgundy a most pleasurable place to visit.

There were vineyards planted in Burgundy at the end of the Roman period, but it was the monks in the Middle Ages who really expanded the grape growing. In fact, Burgundy, along with Yorkshire, has to be one of the places to go to for sad people like me who like visiting abbeys. Those at Pontigny, Fontenay and Cluny are all worth seeing. Towards the end of the Middle Ages Burgundy became very wealthy, part of the legacy of which is the beautiful Flemish-inspired architecture. The Hôtel-Dieu in Beaune (pictured on page 13) is a wonderful example, and was once actually the city's hospital. Its founder and first benefactor was Nicolas Rolin, chancellor to two of the Dukes of Burgundy. His generosity started the tradition in Burgundy of donating vineyards to the hospital. In fact, the Hospices de Beaune still receives money from the annual auction of wines made from vineyards which have been bequeathed to it over the centuries.

As will be revealed during our trundle around France, the style and quality of a wine are determined by natural influences, combined with the skill and hard work of humans. Burgundy's greatness is linked to a particularly favourable combination of natural factors affecting the grape growing. The climate is not hot, but neither is it as cold as in the borderline wine-growing regions of Alsace and Champagne, allowing Burgundy to make both great white and great red wines. Its eastern, inland location, away from the moderating effects of the Atlantic Ocean, does, however, lead to more extremes of weather than are found in maritime regions like Bordeaux. Spring frost can be a problem, as can hail in the summer.

What the Burgundians would claim as the ultimate natural blessing is their soil. Many French grape growers have an almost religious belief in the way soil can influence wine quality. However, of all French wine regions, it is Burgundy where one could say that soil has the biggest effect on wine quality (and therefore price). The rock underneath most of Burgundy is limestone. In fact, there are several different layers of limestone which come to the surface in the Burgundy vineyards. What is more, these rocks have mixed with various other deposits to produce a large number of related, but subtly different, soils. This creates the extraordinary situation in Burgundy where two adjoining vineyards that look indistinguishable to a casual observer can produce wines which differ in price by a factor of ten.

The wines of Burgundy

The basic appellation (see 'French wine law' page 60) covering the whole of Burgundy is AC Bourgogne. The dry white version is made from the Chardonnay grape, and the red from the Pinot Noir. However, Burgundy's vineyards are located in several discrete districts, each of which has its own appellation.

Chablis

Right up in the north of Burgundy, within a couple of hours drive of Paris, is Chablis. This large village is responsible for producing one of the world's most famous dry white wines. Visiting Chablis for the first time is a bit of a shock. Market day aside, Chablis is a sleepy sort of place, the only hint of what it is about being the odd sign to some of the cellars, and an occasional glimpse of vineyards from the main street. Yet the wine produced in Chablis is known all around the world and graces the wine lists of most top restaurants.

Chablis is perhaps the most famous wine made from the Chardonnay grape. However, it would be interesting to know how many Chablis drinkers actually realise that they are enjoying a Chardonnay. In fact, the growers in Chablis, and in the rest of Burgundy for that matter, see the vine as merely a conduit for what really counts – the soil. The village is surrounded by gently rolling hills, down which the

BURGUNDY

(above) The Hôtel-Dieu in Beaune

SOIL

The nature and exact significance of the soil's influence on wine quality remains controversial. The evidence from many of Europe's classic vineyard areas suggests that poor, well-drained soils are often those which generate the finest wines. These poor soils (low in organic matter) limit the growth and yield of the vine, forcing it to focus its energy into ripening the grapes. Thus the adage that quality and quantity are incompatible in wine production. The French term 'terroir' encapsulates the various elements of soil, aspect and climate which influence the vine. Recent research and experience in the comparatively warm areas of the New World, where vines are often planted in fertile soils and subject to irrigation, does, however, suggest that higher yields may be possible without automatically sacrificing quality.

FLOYD UNCORKED

vines are planted. The soil on these slopes is a special type of chalky clay, called Kimmeridgian clay and it is this soil which distinguishes Chablis from any other Chardonnay.

A couple of other factors also have a major bearing on the style of Chablis. Being the northernmost outpost of Burgundy means that Chablis has a distinctly chilly climate. Thus even in a good year the wine will have an elegance and crispness of acidity not really found in any other Chardonnay. In fact, this austerity can come as a bit of a shock if you are used to drinking the rich, fat Chardonnays which are produced in the New World. Reinforcing this distinction is the fact that most Chablis is not matured in oak barrels. Chablis is all about climate and *terroir* (see 'Soil' page 13), rather than fancy tricks in the winery.

This devotion to *terroir* leads the Burgundians to have the most complex system in France for rating their vineyards. Fortunately, in Chablis it is almost comprehensible. When you see a bottle labelled 'Chablis', in other words just carrying the name of the village on the label, what you are looking at is a wine

from an ordinary vineyard. If, by contrast, you see something designated 'Chablis Premier Cru', then the grapes for this wine came from one of the better sites. These vineyards are almost invariably found on slopes, where the vines will benefit from greater exposure to the sun. Should you see something labelled 'Chablis Grand Cru', brace yourself and check your overdraft. The Grand Cru wines come from the best sloping vineyards in the district and sell for the highest price of all.

Côte d'Or

Some 150 kilometres south east of Chablis lies the heart of Burgundy, the Côte d'Or. For devotees of red and white Burgundy, this is holy ground. In fact, until the French Revolution, much of it was actually owned by monastic orders, and in particular the Cistercians. The Côte, or slope, is a gentle south-east-facing escarpment running from Dijon, past the city of Beaune, and ending just beyond the village of Santenay. The land on top of the plateau and the flat land at the bottom of the slope are unsuitable for

The village of Meursault, which produces some of the world's greatest dry white wines

grape growing. Hence all the vineyards lie stretched out along the slope itself. It is along this slope that subtle differences in the steepness of the site, its exposure to the sun, and the composition of the soil, can produce the drastic differences in wine quality and price mentioned earlier. The same sort of vineyard classification is used here as in Chablis. In other words, the best vineyards are rated Grand Cru, good sites are designated Premier Cru, and the ordinary land will just produce a wine carrying the village name.

The northern section of the Côte d'Or is called the Côte de Nuits, the southern section the Côte de Beaune. The Côte de Nuits is almost entirely planted in Pinot Noir, and produces some very fine red wines. Hardened Cabernet Sauvignon and Syrah drinkers can sometimes find these great Pinot Noirs very hard to get along with. A top Côte de Nuits, particularly after some time in bottle, will appear quite pale when compared to an equivalent claret or northern Rhône red. Yet it should still have an intense red fruit character, perhaps overlaid with a certain 'farmyardiness'. Given

such a pale colour, and the fruitiness of the nose, the dryness of the tannins can come as a bit of a shock. Famous wine-producing villages in the Côte de Nuits include Gevrey-Chambertin, Vosne-Romanée and Nuits-Saint-Georges.

The production of the Côte de Beaune is divided between reds and dry whites. In Beaune itself, and in the surrounding villages like Pommard, Volnay and Savigny-lès-Beaune, Pinot Noir remains dominant and so red wines are made. Although they can be very good, the Côte de Beaune reds often do not have the resilient structure of a top Côte de Nuits. Just to the south of Volnay, subtle changes in the soil favour the planting of Chardonnay, rather than Pinot Noir. Here we find the two villages with the reputation for producing the greatest white Burgundies: Meursault and Puligny-Montrachet. The Chardonnay grape in these villages is capable of producing white wines of profound complexity. In fact, if pushed, many people would say that the village of Puligny-Montrachet is responsible for producing the world's finest dry white

wines. Fermentation and maturation of the wines in oak barrels plays its part but *terroir* is, as ever, an important factor. In the extreme south of the Côte de Beaune, around the village of Santenay, the soil changes again and Pinot Noir returns as the main player.

A cautionary note

Before we move on, a word of warning about buying fine Burgundy: to be sure of getting an excellent bottle of wine it is not enough to rely on the village name and the vineyard rating system. After much of the vineyard land had been seized by the State from the monks and aristocrats during the French Revolution, it was auctioned off, often in quite small parcels. Over the last two hundred years, French inheritance law has meant that these small parcels have been further sub-divided. So what had once been a vineyard with one owner is now divided up like a patchwork quilt. Dozens of growers may own tiny plots in what looks like one undivided field. The problem is that each of these growers can, quite legitimately, sell his wine with the name of the field on the label. Some examples will be very good, others could be pretty grim. As a consumer, there is no easy answer to this quandary. The best advice with Burgundy is always to take note of the name of the grower, or merchant (*négociant*) whose wine(s) you have enjoyed. If you liked a grower's Pommard, there is a good chance that you will also like his Volnay. Taking a gamble that a different producer's Pommard will be as good as the first one is much riskier.

(left) Eroded Burgundian vineyard

(right) Have you ever been gripped by limestone?

Côte Chalonnaise

Just south of the Côte d'Or is a district called the Côte Chalonnaise. Reds and dry whites, made from the Pinot Noir and Chardonnay respectively, are produced here. Whilst not as fine as the wines of the Côte d'Or, the good news is that the wines of the Côte Chalonnaise are moderately priced. The appellations of Mercurey, Givry and Rully cover both reds and dry whites, whereas that of Montagny is just for dry whites. As well as the Chardonnay, this district also grows another white grape called the Aligoté. This variety produces a rather crisp, acid, dry white wine. It has its own appellation, AC Bourgogne Aligoté. Some sparkling wine is also made in this district, again with its own designation, AC Crémant de Bourgogne. Based on a blend of Chardonnay and

Pinot Noir and produced by the *méthode traditionelle* (traditional method - see the chapter on Champagne, page 126) this can offer very good value for money.

Mâconnais

A short distance south again brings one to the Mâconnais. The AC Mâcon covers dry whites made from the Chardonnay and light reds made from the Gamay. The Mâconnais whites are generally much superior to the reds, and in fact the top white wine villages have their own designation, AC Mâcon-Villages. If a wine comes from a single village, its name sometimes replaces the 'Villages' on the wine label, for example Mâcon-Lugny. Right down in the south of the Mâconnais are the two top white wine appellations in the district, Pouilly-Fuissé and Saint-Véran.

Beaujolais

A final hop south lands one in Beaujolais. Although included in Burgundy, in many ways Beaujolais is quite a different beast. Firstly, Beaujolais is made from the Gamay grape, rather than the Pinot Noir which rules the roost in the Côte d'Or. The Gamay produces fruity, quaffing, red wines, which are usually quite light in tannins. Secondly, the limestone subsoil, which has underlain the Burgundy vineyards all the way from Chablis to the Mâconnais, is replaced by granite in the best Beaujolais vineyards. It is also worth remembering that ever since leaving Chablis we have been travelling south, so by the time Beaujolais is reached the climate is considerably warmer than it was further north. They even train the vines in a different way from elsewhere in Burgundy: rather than training them along wires, in Beaujolais the vines are traditionally trained up posts.

The basic appellation is just AC Beaujolais, a simple wine with a deep pink colour, lots of fruit on the palate and very little tannin. Many people's first encounter with Beaujolais is through a variation of this wine, Beaujolais Nouveau. This very light red wine is released for drinking on the third Thursday of

November each year, some two months after the grapes were picked. Most red wines are undrinkable at this stage (cynics would say that Beaujolais Nouveau is as well). However, because the Gamay grape does not contain much tannin, and because of a trick in the winemaking called carbonic maceration (see 'Red winemaking' page 56-7), it is possible to produce a simple glugging red wine for early release. Drink up quickly – Beaujolais Nouveau is so light and low in tannin that it does not keep well.

One step up from AC Beaujolais is AC Beaujolais-Villages. As with Mâcon-Villages, Beaujolais-Villages will come from the better villages in the district.

Finally, there are ten villages which are judged to make the best Beaujolais. Each of these villages has its own appellation, and so the village name appears on the label, rather than any mention of Beaujolais. These top villages are often referred to as being the 'Beaujolais Crus'. The ten are as follows: Brouilly, Chénas, Chiroubles, Côte de Brouilly, Fleurie, Juliénas, Morgon, Moulin-à-Vent, Regnié and Saint-Amour. With more concentration and structure than regular Beaujolais, which should be enjoyed while fresh and fruity, the best examples of these 'Cru' wines will keep for a few years.

Grape varieties

The species of vine which is generally cultivated for wine production is *Vitis vinifera*, the European vine. Although wine can be made from various species of American vine, they are mainly used as rootstocks. Within the species *Vitis vinifera*, there are over a thousand varieties of vine. Like varieties of rose or apple, each one has its own distinctive characteristics. Perhaps most importantly, the grapes produced by the various varieties often have markedly different aromas and flavours. These differences of smell and taste are usually apparent in the finished wines, and provide one of the major distinguishing features between them.

In recent years, the names of the grape varieties used have appeared on the labels of many wines. This has been particularly true in the New World and Eastern Europe, where wines are being marketed from vineyard areas or cultures with which the consumer has had little or no previous contact.

The varieties below, and in each chapter, have emerged as being internationally successful:

CHARDONNAY. Chardonnay is perhaps the best known of all the grape varieties. Its fashionability has resulted in it being planted all around the world. However, its home patch is Burgundy, where it makes great white wines like Chablis and Meursault. It is also one of the grapes used in the blend for Champagne. The flavour characteristics of Chardonnay are hard to define, but it often has a rich, buttery, peachy aroma. On the palate it is not too acid, and can achieve quite high alcohol levels. Unlike many white grapes, Chardonnay works well when aged in oak.

PINOT NOIR. This is the grape responsible for red Burgundy. It is not an easy vine to grow, being susceptible to grey rot. Also, quality is easily compromised by high yields. Compared to many other black grapes, the Pinot Noir is lightly pigmented and therefore its wines are often deceptively pale. However, at its best it can produce orgasmic wines. Outside Burgundy, fine examples of Pinot Noir have been made by individual producers in Oregon, California and South Africa. Pinot Noir is also a crucial component of the Champagne blend.

The Château de Tanlay, near Chablis

FLOYD UNCORKED

How to taste wine

The first thing to do is to relax. People get themselves into a terrible state thinking that wine tasting is some sort of bizarre ritual, accessible only to a chosen few. 'They taste wine, we just drink it' seems to be the feeling a lot of people have. In fact, the process of wine tasting merely expands on what we all do instinctively when eating or drinking.

But why bother? In my experience, you cannot teach someone to like a wine which they find unpleasant. Why not just get on and quaff the stuff? In fact, there are a number of good reasons why it is worth being able to taste wines properly. Firstly, you can spot nuances in a wine which you would not have noticed before. This extra insight can increase your pleasure in a good wine. Secondly, by understanding the smell and flavour of a wine, you can better understand your own tastes. For instance, you may personally find Muscadet too sharp and tart, in which case it may be worth trying white wines which are less acid, or have a hint of sweetness. Understanding the smell and flavour of wine also helps when you are trying to match food and wine. Your choice of wine becomes less arbitrary, and you should have fewer disappointing bottles. Thirdly, by keeping a tasting note, you can

check back on wines you have tasted in the past, and this can help to inform your current buying decisions. It can also be pleasant to be reminded of fine bottles enjoyed in the past.

The three senses used when tasting wine are sight, smell and taste.

The first thing to check on the appearance of a wine is clarity. If a wine is cloudy or dull, there is a good chance that there is something wrong with it. Assuming the wine is bright and clear, go on to look at the intensity of the colour. For instance, amongst white wines, Sauternes has a deep colour while Pouilly-Fumé tends to be quite pale. This of course requires a bit of practice, until you know the full range of colour intensities. You then need to describe the colour. Sauternes, for example, as well as having a deep colour, is usually quite golden in appearance. With red wines, as well as noting the colour in the centre of your glass, which can vary from an opaque purpley-black to tawny red, it is also worth tilting the glass and looking at the rim – the shallow, upper edge of the wine. Young red wines are purple and pink on the rim. With a little age, the colour goes to ruby. Further maturation will turn the rim colour more towards brick red, whilst in very old red wines it will be tawny. The rim can be quite narrow, with the central body of saturated colour reaching right up to the edge, or, at the other extreme, broad and watery. Both white and red wines may produce what are known as 'legs' or oily-looking tears running down the side of the glass when it is swirled. This usually suggests a high alcohol content, but may also reflect the sugar level.

Give your wine glass a good swirl to release more aroma. Then snort away. As with the appearance, the first thing to check is whether the wine smells clean and fresh, i.e., is 'correct' and not faulty in any way. If it smells mouldy, or in some other way revolting, you have at least saved yourself the agony of putting the wine in your mouth. Assuming the wine is sound, try to gauge the intensity of the wine's smell. As on the appearance, this will require a little practice to 'calibrate' your nose. A wine like Rosé d'Anjou usually has a light aroma intensity, as opposed to something like the white Alsace Gewürztraminer which can be very pungent. You then have the challenge of trying to define the smell. One rough way to get started is to look for four main families of smell: fruity, floral, vegetal and earthy. Some wines show all four, but very often one stands out (usually fruit). If you get a fruit aroma, just try to push it one stage further and think what type. One of the magic things about wine is that although it is made from grapes, you can often smell hints of many other fruits. You can finish the nose stage by looking out for any oak smells on the wine.

Now you finally get to taste the wine. The first thing to check is whether the wine contains any sugar. If you cannot detect any sweetness,

then the wine is described as being 'dry'. Some sweetness would make the wine 'medium', and a lot of sugar makes it 'sweet'.

The second thing to try to gauge is acidity. Some wines, like Alsace Riesling, are naturally high in acidity, whereas others like Côtes du Lubéron are low.

The third thing to get a fix on is the wine's alcohol content, most noticeable by the warm glow it produces in the mouth and throat. Normal wines can vary from 7.5% alcohol by volume (ABV) right up to 15% ABV. You can check your accuracy by looking at the label.

When tasting a red wine you should also think about the wine's tannin content. Tannins are extracted from the skins of black grapes, and give red wines their earthy, chewy, astringent flavour and what is called their structure or 'backbone'. Médoc wines tend to contain a lot of tannins, whereas Beaujolais doesn't.

With all wines, it is worth holding the wine in your mouth for a few moments before swallowing. If you do this, you will notice that some wines are heavy and rich in the mouth, whereas others are light and delicate. The former can be described as being full bodied, the latter as light bodied.

The final thing to consider is how long the flavour of the wine persists in your mouth after swallowing – that is, the length of finish. The flavour of great wines should linger in your mouth for a very long time.

FLOYD UNCORKED

Wine glasses

Craftsmen have been creating beautiful, and in some cases hideous, wine glasses for hundreds of years. Often the most ornate and exquisite glasses are totally inappropriate for wine tasting. Coloured glasses should be avoided, nor is cut glass ideal, as both types make observing the wine's appearance difficult. The ideal tasting glass is a plain tulip shape, with a fairly long stem. The tulip-shaped bowl of the glass allows the wine to be swirled, and the narrowing top concentrates the aroma. The long stem means the glass can be held without finger marks getting on to the bowl, or body heat altering the wine's smell. Most people in the wine trade around the world use a small glass in the shape described, which is the official ISO Tasting Glass. For people fascinated by such things, there are companies who design special glasses to suit different types of wine. Perhaps of more relevance to most of us is the need always to check that the glasses being used for tasting have no smell. A glass that smells of detergent or cardboard is not going to help show off any sort of wine.

Serving wine

Having sorted out your glassware, the next task is to serve the wine in such a way as to gain most pleasure from drinking it. The main issue is service temperature. Everyone has heard that white wine should be served chilled and red wine at room temperature. The trouble is that people go to extremes in both cases. The result is white wines that are so chilled one might as well suck an ice-lolly, and reds that are so warm that the addition of a few spices would produce mulled wine. For most white and rosé wines 8°C, and for red wines around 17°C, would be about right. Some light red wines, like Beaujolais, can be served a bit cooler than this, say 12°C. Sparkling wines, and some very sweet wines, should be served chilled right down to 4°C. If unsure, err slightly on the cool side as wines tend to

warm up quite quickly in the glass.

Something consumers do not often realise is that at many wine trade tastings all the wines are served at room temperature. Although this approach is not very flattering to a white wine, it does give you a 'warts and all' impression of the wine's characteristics.

It is worth bearing in mind that even professionals differ sometimes on what is an ideal temperature. A producer in Burgundy insisted on serving his white wines at 14°C so as to show off the wines' nuances. To me, though, this temperature over-exaggerated the vegetal aromas, spoiling the overall balance.

Another piece of wine lore is that red wines should be opened well before being served, maybe a

couple of hours, to allow them to 'breathe'. Some people swear by this technique, others feel it has little effect on the wine. The argument goes that the air contact makes a young red wine taste a bit smoother. However, the act of pouring wine into a glass, and the air contact the wine subsequently has in-between sips of wine, will also let the wine breathe pretty well. Probably the best approach is to try for yourself whether your favourite red wines are improved by being left to breathe. Be careful with old red wine though – the shock of contact with the air can cause rapid deterioration.

Wine tasting notes

I drink whisky, I drink beer, I drink wine. I love fatty pork and beef on the bone. I eat chocolate, fish and chips and caviar and drink vodka. I drink instant coffee but adore a Spanish café solo. I eat chillies, ginger and garlic. I adore pungent blue cheeses like Roquefort and Gorgonzola and Danish blue. I love liver with fried onions and I enjoy ice cream with hot chocolate sauce between cigarettes. I drink Champagne on occasion, aquavit rarely, gin and tonic occasionally. I love apples and Mars bars. In fact I am a chocoholic. Actually I am a kind of gastronomic tramp. I am too hungry for dinner at eight, and sometimes at breakfast a curry is great. Ossobuco in an Italian service station can please, an ignorantly served hamburger can bring you to your knees. For me the whole thing about eating and drinking is whatever gives you pleasure, enjoyment and fun.

I have no doubt that my brief reflections on some of the wines I have been drinking for many years will contrast strikingly with the erudite views of our esteemed Master of Wine, Jonathan Pedley. So, here are my views, highly personal, not academic, just what I think.

I feel I should emphasise that these notes are based on our tasting sessions, and reflect Keith's and my own reactions to specific wines. When you come to taste equivalent wines (probably from a different producer and/or a different year) you may well disagree with some of our descriptions. No matter. It simply highlights the importance of factors like producer and vintage, and how they affect the quality and style of the wine.

CHABLIS

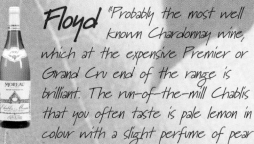

Floyd "Probably the most well known Chardonnay wine, which at the expensive Premier or Grand Cru end of the range is brilliant. The run-of-the-mill Chablis that you often taste is pale lemon in colour with a slight perfume of pear drops and a conflicting, crisp apple flavour. I am not sure New World wines simply labelled as 'Chardonnay' from Australia, California or South Africa will not please more."

Pedley "Clear and bright. Pale lemon colour. Very clean and fresh. Moderate intensity of smell. Youthful, with a whiff of peardrops. Fruity. A hint of apple. Dry, with high acidity and moderate alcohol. Fairly light bodied. Moderate length of finish."

SAVIGNY-LES-BEAUNE

Floyd "Savigny-lès-Beaune is one of the mid-ranking villages in the Côte de Beaune. It is a reliable, general purpose red which will neither disappoint nor surprise but is happily drinkable with almost all food. In my view, it is overrated because it is a popular name but without the quality to match. A Côte de Nuits such as Nuits-Saint-Georges might please you better."

Pedley "Medium depth of ruby red in the body. Fairly narrow pink rim, with just a hint of orange. Clean, with a moderate intensity of smell. Lots of red fruit character. Redcurrants, cherries, raspberries. Some oakiness is present as well. On the palate the wine is dry, with moderate acidity and warm alcohol. The tannins are quite noticeable but not rasping. Not particularly heavy, rather mid-bodied. Quite a long finish."

POUILLY-FUISSE

Pedley "Bright greenish straw. Quite an intense ripe nose. Peach and pineapple. Underlying oily weight. A slightly floral edge as well. Dry, mid-high acidity, high alcohol. Mid to light-bodied. Warm and open. Reasonably long finish."

FLEURIE

Pedley "Darkish purple body. Mid-breadth pink rim. Moderately intense, perfumed nose. Tinned fruits, in particular strawberries. Juicy and jammy. Dry, lowish acidity, fairly high alcohol. Very light tannins. Light body. Moderate length of finish."

Floyd food notes

Burgundy is a big region with four *départements* – Yonne, Nièvre, the Côte d'Or and Saône-et-Loire. It also has three important rivers: the Rhône, the Saône and, of course, the gushing River of Beaujolais. From the drinker's point of view, the Côte d'Or is the most important area of Burgundy, as this is where the really expensive and extravagant wines come from: Corton, Chambertin, Echézeaux, Le Montrachet and Le Musigny, to name but a few. Of course, a lot of good wine is also made around Mâcon, Chalon and Mercurey, not forgetting Beaujolais.

I dimly recall a very thoughtful day spent tasting Gevrey-Chambertin in a small and totally traditional cellar in the village of the same name, and I vaguely remember, that same evening, discovering for the first time (this is many years ago, by the by) a drink called *Kir Cardinale*. Not the now ubiquitous blackcurrant liqueur made famous by Mayor Kir of Dijon, who added Crème de Cassis to a light white Burgundy wine. No. The huge, hand-blown glass of deep vermillion wine, handed to me by the châtelaine in the manor house where I was staying, was the full-leaded Monty! It was 1961 Gevrey-Chambertin poured over a generous splash of double-concentrated Crème de Cassis. A light supper of Burgundian snails in a parsley and garlic cream, followed by *Oeufs en Meurette* (eggs poached in red wine) and then *Andouillettes* (chitterling sausages) cooked in Chablis, was washed down with a magnum of Chambertin. (A magnum, to my way of thinking, is a little too much for one but not quite enough for two.)

Somewhere around the *Poires Belle Dijonnaise* – a superb confection of pears and Crème de Cassis – or was it after the Explorateur cheese, or possibly during the Vieux Marc de Bourgogne, I came up with this brilliant idea to make a fortune; or at least I think I did – the trouble with that evening was, as I recall, (to misquote Bob Dylan) 'I had started out on Burgundy, but soon hit the harder stuff...' Anyway, the nub of my wizard money-making scheme was to invent a wine-drinker's board game, which, needless to say, I have copyrighted, called 'Vinopoly'. You see, the day before, or perhaps it was the following day, I don't really remember, I had driven through the most expensive wine list in the world; unfortunately, in a mere turbo-charged Volvo, not ideally suited to driving through the villages of Beaune, Gevrey-Chambertin, Nuits-Saint-Georges, Aloxe-Corton, Meursault, Vosne-Romanée, etc, etc. However, I digress.

Some classic dishes of Burgundy include wonderful roast *Poulet de Bresse* with truffles, *Boeuf Bourguignon, Coq au Vin, Pochouse* – a creamy stew of freshwater fish, and virtually anything cooked in Chablis or Dijon mustard. If you want to try some really exquisite snails cooked in parsley and garlic cream, go to Bernard Morillon's restaurant in Beaune, or if you fancy pig's trotters stuffed with mustard, try the Ermitage de Corton on the Dijon road out of Beaune. I first tasted *Jambon Persillé*, an exquisite dish of jellied ham with chopped parsley, in a restaurant called Pré aux Clercs (so named because it is near the church) in Dijon over thirty years ago. Like Hiély in Provence it still retains its Michelin star and is dishing up excellent food.

The point about my board game, by the way, is you get to drink at all those places, but you don't have to drive, just throw the dice. Bonne Santé!

Saupiquet de jambon
(Ham in Chablis and mustard sauce)

6 generous slices of cooked, slightly smoked ham, off the bone if possible (unsmoked ham is also **OK**)

100 g/3½ oz butter

dash of olive oil

3 or 4 shallots, very finely diced

500 g/1 lb 2 oz button mushrooms, very finely sliced

3 or 4 glasses of Chablis

approximately 150 ml/¼ pint chicken or veal stock

about 1 tablespoon smooth Dijon mustard

about 1 tablespoon grainy Dijon-style mustard

100 ml/3½ fl oz double cream

a good knob of butter

salt and pepper

Serves 4-6

Heat some of the butter and oil in a heavy frying or sauté pan and cook the shallots and mushrooms until the shallots are golden and just beginning to caramelise lightly. Add the white wine, turn up the heat and reduce the liquid by half. Then add the chicken or veal stock and bubble away for 3 or 4 minutes. Reduce the heat to a simmer and stir in the mustard carefully so as not to damage the mushrooms. When the mustard is well amalgamated with the liquid, stir in the cream gently over a low heat, taste and season with salt and pepper. If the sauce is either a little too thin or too strongly flavoured, reduce gently and carefully stir in some little knobs of butter which will amalgamate, thicken and enrich the sauce.

Just before the sauce is ready, warm the ham quickly by frying on both sides in a hot pan with the remaining butter and oil. Pour the sauce over the ham. Serve with fresh pasta noodles (not the traditional accompaniment, but they go brilliantly with this dish) and a really crisp, mixed leaf salad.

Recommended wine – Chablis

Coq au vin

(Cockerel in red wine)

1 cockerel, approximately 2 kilos/4½lb (with liver and giblets)
2 tablespoons plain flour
125 g/4½ oz butter
half a wine glass of olive oil
200 g/7 oz thick-cut smoked bacon diced into small cubes
20 small onions, peeled
4 garlic cloves, crushed
1 large glass of Marc de Bourgogne (spirit made from the residues of Burgundy wine fermentation)
at least 1 litre/1¼ pints red Burgundy
1 bouquet garni
1 tablespoon sugar
1 wine glass of poultry blood or 100 g/3½ oz soft boudin noir (black blood sausage) plus a little olive oil
200 g/7 oz small button mushrooms
salt and pepper

Serves 4

This dish is designed to make good use of a farmyard cockerel. An elderly hen would also be fine, but you may have to make do with a capon. Do what you can to get hold of a cockerel, however, as the dish will be very much better for it.

Joint the bird into 8 pieces and toss the pieces in the flour. Fry the chicken in some of the butter and oil in a large casserole until the chicken starts to colour. Add the bacon, the onions and the garlic and continue cooking until the onions begin to colour. Now flame the lot with the Marc de Bourgogne. When the flames have died down pour in the red wine and add the bouquet garni and salt and pepper. Add the giblets to the pot (also the liver if you're not using it later to thicken the stew), bring quickly to the boil, add the sugar, reduce the heat to a very, very slow simmer and cover the pot. Cook for approximately 1½ to 2 hours, until the chicken is tender.

If you don't have any poultry blood, remove the skin from the boudin and chop the sausage into small pieces. Dice the reserved liver and place it into a blender or processor bowl along with the boudin and a little olive oil and purée. Remove the giblets and the bouquet garni from the casserole and discard, then stir in the liver and boudin mixture. If you are using poultry blood, remove the casserole from the heat before whisking in the blood. The casserole can be returned to the heat for a minute or two but must not boil. Check the seasoning, adding salt and pepper if necessary.

Ten minutes before serving the dish, sauté the button mushrooms in the remaining butter and oil until they are very well cooked, season with salt and pepper and add to the casserole just before serving.

Recommended wine – red Côte de Beaune

LOIRE VALLEY

Pays Nantais ⸺ Anjou-Saumur ⸺ Touraine ⸺ Central Vineyards

SAVENNIÈRES

ANJOU

ST.-NICOLAS-
DE-BOURGUEIL

VOUVRAY

Orléans

Loire   Gien

Angers

BOURGUEIL

Blois

POUILLY-
FUMÉ

St.-Nazaire

Loire

Vouvray

SANCERRE

Nantes

COTEAUX
DU
LAYON

Loire

Saumur

Tours

Cher

MENETOU
SALON

Sancerre

MUSCADET

SAUMUR

Indre

QUINCY

Pouilly-sur-
Loire

MUSCADET DE
SÈVRE-ET-MAINE

SAUMUR-
CHAMPIGNY

CHINON

REUILLY

Bourges

THE LOIRE WINE REGION

LOIRE

*T*he River Loire takes a majestic sweep through the middle of France. Starting a long way south near Le Puy, for the first half of its journey to the sea it is graced by few vineyards. Then, as it changes direction from due north to due west, the vineyards appear, and accompany it virtually all the way to the Atlantic Ocean.

It is not only vineyards that appear at this stage of the river's course; many of the famous châteaux associated with the Loire Valley can be found around Tours. Each of these châteaux has its own charms, but the position of Chenonceau (seen here), spanning the River Cher, and the delicacy of its architecture, make it a very special place.

The location of the Loire vineyards, quite a long way north in France, means that they experience a fairly cool climate. In these conditions, wines will be produced that are high in acidity, with a delicacy of fruit and lightness of body. Such elements in a wine usually suit white wines, and it is this style which dominates the Loire's production.

A cool northern climate, influenced by the relative proximity of the Atlantic Ocean, makes for very changeable weather through the growing season. A reasonably warm summer and dry autumn are important if Loire wines are to show at their best. If the summer is cool and the autumn wet, the wines can be pretty thin and acid.

The wines of the Loire

For wine purposes, the Loire is normally divided up into four districts. Running from west to east these are: Nantais, Anjou-Saumur, Touraine and Central Vineyards, a span of some 400 kilometres. Across such a long distance there are quite marked differences of soil, and although all the Loire districts share a cool climate, factors like rainfall vary from vineyard to vineyard.

Nantais

The Nantais is the westernmost outpost of the Loire, lying just inside the border of Brittany. This cool, wet district produces one of France's most famous dry white wines, Muscadet. As well as being dry, Muscadet tends to be very high in acidity and only moderate in alcohol. The fruit character is often tart and green. Muscadet is unusual amongst French wines in actually being the name of the grape used to make the wine, rather than that of the district or village where the wine is made. The basic designation for the wine is simply AC Muscadet. Within the Nantais, probably the best area for growing the Muscadet vine lies south east of the city of Nantes. The two little rivers flowing through this area are the River Sèvre and the River Maine. They give their name to the superior designation, AC Muscadet de Sèvre et Maine. Regular Muscadet can be rather neutral in character. One way

to get more flavour in the wine involves an interesting trick in the winemaking. Instead of racking the newly fermented white wine straight after fermentation (see 'White winemaking', page 34-5), top Muscadets are left resting on the yeast lees during the winter. Having spent around six months in contact with the yeast, the wine will only then be racked and bottled. This

Bud burst in a Muscadet vineyard

earns the wine an AC with a further qualifier: Muscadet de Sèvre et Maine Sur Lie. Maturation on the lees gives the wine a bready, yeasty aroma. Sur Lie Muscadets often also contain a little dissolved carbon dioxide left over from the fermentation. This does not make them sparkling as such, but tiny carbon dioxide bubbles sometimes form on the glass when the wine is served.

Anjou-Saumur

Anjou-Saumur is most famous for its rosé wine. The AC Rosé d'Anjou covers fairly simple, inexpensive, medium dry rosés. A blend of local black grapes is used, based around the sinister sounding Groslot. The popularity of Anjou Rosé rather overshadows the district's other wines, which is a shame as some of them are very good. The star local white grape is the Chenin Blanc. Anjou Blanc is the basic white wine appellation, and like the rosé this often appears as a medium dry wine. Some very classy dry white wines are, however, produced from the Chenin Blanc in the tiny area of AC Savennières, whilst, by way of contrast, the AC Coteaux du Layon produces very fine sweet white wines. The Chenin Blanc grape retains high acidity even when ripe. This, combined with the Loire's cool climate, means that Coteaux du Layon tends to be fresher and less oily than Sauternes. Unfortunately, as with Savennières, the production of Coteaux du Layon is very small.

Although AC Saumur covers most styles of wine, the town is most famous for its production of sparkling whites. These are made by the traditional method, but differ markedly from Champagne in being based on Chenin Blanc. Given their moderate price, they generally offer good value for money. Reaching right up to the border with Touraine is the appellation Saumur-Champigny, producing red wines, something for which the Loire is not particularly well known. In a warm summer, however, when black grapes can ripen properly, some decent, and occasionally a few fine red wines can be made in the Loire. Their charm will always be based on elegance and freshness, rather than on richness or structure. The key quality black grape in the Loire is the Cabernet Franc. In Bordeaux, the Cabernet Franc usually plays an accompanying role to Cabernet Sauvignon and Merlot, but in the Loire it often takes a solo part.

CLIMATE

If grape variety is the single most important factor in determining a wine's aroma, then climate is usually the most important in determining its structure. Climate certainly determines the viability of grape growing. The vine needs temperate conditions, with a cool winter period followed by a warm summer, and ideally a moderate amount of natural rainfall. For this reason, virtually all the world's vineyards are located in the bands of latitude 30°–50°N and 30°–50°S.

However, within these bands of latitude, there are quite markedly varied climates, each exerting its own subtle influence. Grapes growing in a cool climate, for instance, even when reasonably ripe, retain high levels of acidity and achieve only moderate concentrations of sugar. The crisp acidity of the grapes will be discernible in the finished wine, and the moderate concentration of grape sugar will give only moderate levels of alcohol after fermentation. Such wines will tend to be elegant rather than overpowering, their naturally high acidity making them ideal partners for many types of food. Conversely, the high sugar levels found in grapes grown in hot areas will give wines which are high in alcohol. These wines are often rich and round, but risk lacking acidity and finesse.

White winemaking

After harvesting, the grapes are transported from the vineyard to the winery as quickly as possible. This is important as they can deteriorate quickly if left in contact with the air. When the grapes arrive at the winery the batch is weighed, and a sample is taken for analysis.

GRAPE STRUCTURE

Pulp: sugar, acids (tartaric and malic), water

Stalk: harsh tannins

Pips: bitter oils

Skin: colour, tannins, flavour

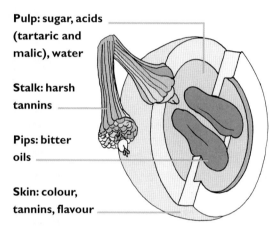

White wine is usually made from white grapes. The first stage in the winemaking process involves crushing and destalking the grapes. Because of the harsh tannins in the stalks, it makes sense to eliminate them at the beginning of the production process. The crushed grapes are then dropped into a press. The press is switched on and the grape juice (also known as 'must') is squeezed out. Once most of the juice has been extracted, the press is opened, the mass of grapes broken up, and the press activated for a second time. The juice from this 'Second Pressing' will be rougher than that from the 'First Pressing'. These two fractions will usually be fermented separately, and then later on the winemaker can decide what should be blended with what.

The juice is allowed to settle for a few hours, and its sugar content is checked. If there is insufficient natural grape sugar in the juice, then refined sugar can be added at this stage (a process called 'chaptalisation'). It is also normal practice to add a small amount of sulphur dioxide to the must. Sulphur dioxide has been used for centuries in winemaking to kill bacteria (preventing the juice turning to vinegar) and moulds, and as an anti-oxidant.

The juice now ferments. The traditional approach is to leave the vats of juice for a matter of hours, or sometimes days, and rely on natural yeast to start the fermentation. These indigenous yeast may be present on the grape skins, on winery equipment, or in the atmosphere. Relying on the natural yeast can be a bit of a gamble as many different strains of yeast exist, some of which produce unpleasant smells. However, many winemakers in France would argue that natural yeast are one of the sources of a wine's character, and in a way are as much a part of 'terroir' as the soil or microclimate. By contrast, the modern approach to fermentation would be to add a specially selected cultured yeast to the must. Cultured yeast give a clean fermentation and are very reliable.

During fermentation the yeast turn the grape sugar into alcohol (ethanol) and carbon dioxide. For the anoraks, the chemical equation is:

$$C_6H_{12}O_6 \rightarrow 2C_2H_5OH + 2CO_2 + \text{Heat}$$

Sugar → Ethanol + Carbon dioxide

As anyone who has fermented their own beer or wine knows, in addition to alcohol and carbon dioxide, the process generates a lot of heat. If the heat is not dissipated, the wine can suffer a loss of fruitiness. As the temperature approaches 35°C the yeast die, stopping the fermentation and opening the way for bacteria to destroy the wine.

Temperature-controlled stainless steel vats – ubiquitous now in wineries all the way from Marlborough to Mâcon

The answer is to control the fermentation temperature, for most white wines keeping it in the range of 15°C–20°C. Many wineries achieve this by fermenting their wines in temperature-controlled stainless steel vats. These are incredibly unromantic, but by running cold water down the outside of the vats, or through an exterior jacket, the temperature inside can be kept under control. Stainless steel also has the advantage of being easy to clean. Some top white wines, however, particularly those made from the Chardonnay grape, will be fermented in oak barrels.

It takes about two weeks for all the sugar to be used up and for the fermentation process to end. The yeast then slowly sink to the bottom of the vat, forming a sediment known as 'lees'.

Whilst resting on the lees, wine can undergo a second transformation. One of the acids found in grapes is malic acid, which has a very sharp, tart, green flavour. Naturally occurring bacteria in the lees can convert this 'appley' acid into the softer, more 'milky' lactic acid. This natural process, called malolactic fermentation, makes a wine less acid, and tends to give it a rounder flavour. Nowadays this process can be controlled, so those winemakers looking to soften their wine and give it an added dimension of flavour encourage it, while others, whose primary concern is to retain a crisp acidity and immediate fruit flavours, block the process.

At the end of the fermentations the wine can be drained off its lees, a process called 'racking'. The wine will then be matured as required.

Touraine

The most famous appellation in the Touraine district
is Vouvray, which benefits from a particular subsoil,
chalk tuffeau – a type of chalk affected by volcanic
activity. The AC is for white wine, and as in Anjou-
Saumur the grape variety used is the Chenin Blanc.
Vouvray is made in almost all conceivable styles: there
are dry, medium and sweet versions, and, in addition,
sparkling and semi-sparkling.

Touraine also makes some everyday dry white
wines from the Sauvignon Blanc, which are sold
under the appellation covering the whole district,
AC Touraine.

At the western end of Touraine, bordering
Saumur-Champigny, are three more red wine only
appellations: Chinon, Bourgueil and Saint-Nicolas-de-
Bourgueil are lightish reds, based, like Saumur-
Champigny, on the Cabernet Franc.

Central Vineyards

The easternmost district in the Loire is the Central
Vineyards, an area of chalky clay with flinty outcrops.
It is here that the Sauvignon Blanc is at its most
expressive in France. The dry white wines of AC
Sancerre and AC Pouilly-Fumé have a massive
following, despite being far from cheap nowadays.
Compared to the Sauvignon Blancs produced in New
Zealand, these Loire wines are generally leaner and
more austere. AC Sancerre covers the production of
red wines as well as whites. It is not far from the
Central Vineyards to Burgundy, so discovering that the
black grape used is Pinot Noir should come as no
surprise. Red Sancerre, however, tends to be much
lighter in body than red Burgundy. There are three
other less well known appellations within the Central
Vineyards, capable of producing decent dry white
wines made from Sauvignon Blanc: Quincy, Reuilly and
Menetou Salon.

WEATHER

**The overall climate of an area changes little
with time. However, weather patterns can
change markedly from year to year. A frost in
the spring, or poor weather at flowering time,
can significantly reduce crop size. Most
importantly, too much rain and/or insufficient
warmth in the weeks immediately preceding
harvest can force the grower to pick grapes
which are unripe and perhaps diseased. Such
grapes will at best only produce ordinary wine.**

**Hence the size and quality of harvest will
vary from one year to the next. The wine
business tends to use the word 'vintage'
instead of the word 'harvest'. Many wines show
their vintage date on the label – useful
information but not an automatic guarantee of
good wine.**

*Trimming the vines in Vouvray
by machine during the summer*

Grape varieties

CHENIN BLANC. Chenin Blanc shares with Riesling the capacity to produce a very broad range of wine styles. In the Loire it is used to make dry, medium and sweet white wines, as well as some good sparkling and semi-sparkling wines. All are under-pinned by very high acidity. In the warmer conditions of South Africa, the Chenin Blanc is the principal white variety, usually producing straightforward, comparatively neutral white wines.

SAUVIGNON BLANC (also known as Fumé Blanc). Although not quite as trendy as Chardonnay, Sauvignon Blanc does have many fans around the world. New Zealand has built a very good reputation for its Sauvignon Blanc, but many people would say that its classic rendition is in the Loire Valley, where it is the grape responsible for Sancerre and Pouilly-Fumé. The aroma of Sauvignon Blanc is very distinctive, having a sharp, grassy, green fruit character, often reminiscent of gooseberries. As well as being dry, most Sauvignon Blancs are very high in acidity.

Seasons in the vineyard

WINTER: The vine lies dormant during the winter months. Cold weather is beneficial as many of the pests and diseases are eradicated. Several vineyard regions experience virtually all their rainfall during this season.

   The principal task in the vineyard during the winter is pruning. It is a crucially important, labour-intensive process, regulating as it does the size of the harvest and the overall balance of the vine. Hard pruning will result in a small crop, but the vine will be able to direct all its energy during the summer into ripening just a few bunches of grapes. Such fruit often has an intensely concentrated flavour.

The flowering takes place in May or June

Tying the vine shoots in the summer to keep the vines neat

The vine lies dormant during the winter

Trimming the vines by hand in summer

LOIRE

SPRING: The buds open in March, and thereafter the vines grow quickly. Once bud-burst has taken place, warm weather is desirable to encourage growth. A little rain is good as well. The vines flower at the end of May or early in June and fine weather is important to guarantee a successful flowering.

The battle against pests and diseases starts in the spring and runs on through the summer, usually involving a regular regime of spraying. The vines shoots have to be tied up to keep the vineyard neat and manageable.

Véraison – *the moment when black grapes change colour*

SUMMER: If the flowering went well, tiny grapes will start to form. Warm, dry and sunny weather is then needed to get the grapes to ripen. A little rainfall may be welcome to prevent the vines suffering water stress. The grapes will swell, their acid content will drop, and the concentration of sugar will rise. Up until the end of July all varieties of grape are green, but thereafter colour starts to form in the skins of black grapes (a process called 'véraison').

The vine will continue to produce shoots and leaves throughout the summer. Trimming and shoot positioning may be necessary to manage this growth. Spraying continues. If the crop looks like being very large, some growers will cut away excess bunches, so that the vine's efforts are concentrated in a smaller yield. The French term for this process is 'éclaircissage' or 'vendange verte'.

AUTUMN: By September time the grapes should be virtually ripe (roughly 100 days after flowering).

The culmination of a year's work – the harvest

Dry weather is important at this critical stage to ensure that the grapes are ripe, concentrated and healthy.

The harvesting can then start. The traditional way to pick the grapes is by hand. Whilst this is very expensive, many producers feel that the careful sorting permitted by hand harvesting is worth the investment. Others, however, favour much less labour-intensive machine harvesting.

Once harvested, the vine will harden its wood before the first frost kills the leaves and the vine becomes dormant again.

WINE TASTING NOTES

POUILLY-FUME

Floyd "Some wines demand more words from me, some less. Pouilly-Fumé is a classic, but as with all these things, the more you spend the better you get. The one I tasted was pale in colour, had an apple or possibly peach flavour, was moderate in alcohol and tasted slightly of butterscotch. Just shows you, doesn't it, how absurd it can be to try to define the characteristics of a wine. I sampled this wine with a bunch of men and women whose taste in wine was based mainly on Liebfraumilch and cheap Chianti. The ladies did not like it as it was not sweet enough, the men liked it because it was dry, but I suspect neither party really liked the wine. I do."

Pedley "Pale greenish straw colour. Very clean and crisp. Fairly intense green fruit character. Pears and green melon. Grassy. Some citrus notes as well. Dry, high acidity and fairly high alcohol. Sharp and fresh. Hint of nettles. A real lively zing on the finish."

VOUVRAY

Floyd "Medium priced versions of Vouvray are very agreeable: pale green in colour, a light, airy taste of grapes, not too strong in alcohol, soft and slightly buttery. Someone suggested it tastes slightly of yams! An ideal wine to drink with snacks and canapés or at parties where you are sure of the appreciation of your guests."

Pedley "Palish lemon with just a hint of green. Quite a marked, sappy, musky, slightly vegetal nose. Sour, green apple fruit. Medium sweetness. Very high underlying acidity. Mid-high alcohol. Mid-bodied. Fresh, stalky fruit. Moderate length."

ROSE D'ANJOU

Pedley "Very pale pink body. Broad watery rim. Light, simple, youthful fruit. Quite neutral, but with a hint of peardrops. Medium dry. High, lean acidity. Moderate alcohol. Very light bodied. Some tart fruit flavours. Shortish finish."

MUSCADET DE SEVRE ET MAINE SUR LIE

Pedley "Pale lime colour. Tiny bubbles on the rim of the wine. Very sharp, tart, crisp nose. Lean, green, stony fruit aromas. Just a hint of yeast. Bone dry. Very high acidity. Mid alcohol. Very light and lean on the palate. Fairly short finish."

Floyd food notes

There are only two ways to enjoy and explore the Loire Valley, its châteaux, towns, villages and vineyards. One is to take several sedate weeks touring by road in, say, a convertible Bentley, stopping here and there at the many fine restaurants that the region boasts, and occasionally staying on a farm. The other is to take a boat, as I once did, from St-Nazaire to Nantes, Angers, Saumur, Tours, Blois, Orléans and so on down to Nevers, stopping frequently to enjoy some *rillettes* (potted pork) and a glass or two of lightly chilled Saumur or (perhaps and) Bourgueil. Nibbling on some local *charcuterie* washed down with an excellent, sweet Coteaux du Layon, as you sit in a field, gazing across the poppies at some pretty old town like Angers, you can think yourself part of an impressionist painting.

The trouble with my boat journey down the Loire was that just before Nantes the engine of my boat packed up and a treacherous current swept the poor old craft into a road-bridge and dismasted her. This unplanned interruption also caused severe financial distress and plans to visit certain restaurants had to be shelved, so we spent hours fishing, catching eel, bream, perch and the like. We could afford little else, other than *charcuterie*, bread and wine, but at least it made me aware what a brilliant food resource freshwater fish are. If you cannot be bothered to fish, kill and cook your own eels, you will find a wonderful *Matelote d'Anguilles* at La Roche le Roy in Tours. In Chinon, at Au Plaisir Gourmand, you get a wonderful zander (pike-perch) in a very delicate *beurre blanc* sauce, for which the Loire is famous. A lot of the locals like to drink sweet wines with these fish dishes, but I prefer a slightly chilled Chinon.

Apart from the vineyards, which were not always so prominent in the region, there are hundreds of small, mixed farms rearing chickens or growing asparagus or maize or flowers. As a consequence, the Loire has a fine heritage of country cooking: delicious maize-fed chickens cooked with Pouilly-Fumé, mushrooms, butter and cream; leg of lamb stewed in wine; pig's tail and red bean stew; rabbit soup and many versions of *matelote* (freshwater fish stew).

The Anjou Rosé you find in Britain somehow seems to arrive, to my mind, as an insipid, oversweet wine. And yet – though Provence rosés are my personal favourites – there are some crackingly good rosés made in Anjou. A bottle of sparkling Vouvray tied to a piece of string, bobbing in the river while you idly watch your float, helps the time glide by while circus cows lap in the reeded shallows on the opposite bank, and a man in a faded straw hat drifts by in his peeled-paint wooden punt. Oh, and by the way, with reference to the aforementioned motoring tour of the valley, I do recommend you have the services of a discreet chauffeur, who never forgets the ice, can uncork bottles and pack a good hamper. Bon Voyage!

Poulet sauté à l'Angevine

(Chicken with onions, mushrooms and cream)

1 corn-fed, free-range chicken, approximately 1.75 kg/4 lb

12 small shallots, peeled

200 g/7 oz unsalted butter

juice of one lemon

approximately 500 ml/18 fl oz Pouilly-Fumé or other dry white Loire wine

250 g/9 oz button mushrooms

300 ml/½ pint double cream

1 tablespoon chopped fresh tarragon leaves

1 egg yolk

salt and black pepper

Serves 4

Cut the chicken into 8 pieces. In a large sauté pan fry the chicken along with the shallots in some of the butter until the shallots are golden brown, then turn down the heat, add the lemon juice, and sauté gently for 20 minutes. Now add enough wine to just cover the chicken. Bring to the boil, reduce the heat, cover and simmer gently for about 30 minutes, until the chicken is almost done. Meanwhile, fry the mushrooms in the remaining butter, add to the chicken and simmer for another 10 minutes. Now remove the chicken, mushrooms and shallots to a serving dish and keep warm.

Over a high heat, reduce the wine and juices by half and season with salt and pepper. Reduce the heat and gently whisk in the cream and the tarragon. Now pull the sauce off the heat and thicken it by whisking in, very quickly, the egg yolk. Pour the thickened sauce over the chicken and vegetables (do not attempt to reheat it, or the sauce will curdle) and serve immediately.

Recommended wine –
Pouilly-Fumé

FLOYD'S

I have decided to link together the Rhône Valley, Provence and the Languedoc, and redefine them as Provence, an area part-colonised by the Romans and named Provincia.

Purists, historians, geographers, Masters of Wine who study the precise areas of *Appellations Contrôlées*, know-all journalists, travel writers, fastidious foodies and ex-pats who fiercely believe that their chosen village is unique and consider the goat's cheese from the Drôme to be *terribly* different from that produced in Carcassonne, and those who believe that St-Tropez or Juan-les-Pins are very special places, will not, of course, agree with me.

The Romans, the Phoenicians, the Greeks, the Arabs and the Moors have all left their mark on this ancient, sun-baked and sometimes inhospitable *terroir* where olives and vines cling to precipitous slopes; where sheep and goats nibble at lavender, thyme and rosemary, as do rabbits, wild boar and other game animals; where great rivers like the Rhône create fertile valleys in which soft fruits, artichokes and asparagus flourish.

A hot sun has always dominated blue skies, but when the Mistral blows icy-cold in the winter it is time to prepare a great pot of *cassoulet*. This sumptuous stew is a rib-sticking dish of dried white beans and preserved duck, goose and sausages, to be served day after finger-numbing day of back-aching work tending vines and olive groves or shepherding sheep or goats. Have you ever thought how this classic dish was born out of necessity, out of the need to preserve food before refrigeration? Hence in late summer or early autumn the few ducks or geese that a hill farmer owned were killed and their feathers reserved for stuffing pillows, their blood cooked into little pancakes for enriching soups and stews, while giblets, along with necks and feet and the flesh, were all stewed in their own fat and hermetically sealed in earthenware or glass jars to provide food stores over the winter. Beans were ever a cheap staple. The garlic and tomatoes would be grown in the summer, the garlic then dried and the tomatoes preserved. The pig, too, would have been killed and the sausages made well before winter set in: the fresh blood would have been made into *boudin noir*, black pudding, while sausages would be made from the minced belly and hung in an airy, dry place to cure. The pig's legs would have been soaked in brine, then dried and also hung to cure in order to produce *jambon cru*. The trotters would be used to flavour pulse soups and add richness, nutrients and flavour to an otherwise staple diet of beans and lentils.

Can you imagine coming back from a hard day's labour and eating stewed beans with a little bit of dried sausage and preserved goose or duck – if you were lucky – virtually every day throughout the winter? Yet isn't it even more curious that we eat this winter dish on our summer holidays in France, under a scorching sun and in soaring temperatures? Let's face it, that's what most of us do, because we never go on holiday to such places in the winter, when there is no sun. (However, that's just me wittering on about how stupid tourists can be!) If you want to eat a cassoulet – and it is a magnificent dish – either cook it at home in the winter (you can of course buy your goose or duck ready-preserved as *confit d'oie or de canard*), or go on your hols in the winter. You won't find it in St-Tropez or Juan-les-Pins, but then, as you purists, historians, Masters of Wine *et al* always say, they're not actually in my Provence.

In summer in Provence, that is to say my Provence, go to a village *fête champêtre*. It will usually be on some national holiday like the 14th July, and there will be a boules tournament, maybe water jousting, some truly awful band or maybe a brilliant showband, alternating between Supertramp, Status Quo, Edith Piaf, waltzes, country and western, and those highly warbling romantic French songs like *Chanson d'amour*, on a stage constructed in front of the immaculate monument, draped with the *Tricolore*, honouring the children of France murdered, shot or deported by the Germans in two World Wars. In the square, under the plane trees, there will be long trestle tables and folding chairs and you will eat a *Grand Aïoli* composed of snails, salt cod, boiled potatoes, carrots, artichokes, green beans and hardboiled eggs, all covered in a thick, yellow, garlicky mayonnaise – the aïoli from which the dish takes its name. This is a garrulous feast, washed down with iced rosé wines, or chilled reds mixed with a little water: you will hear tales of the harvest, or the War, or the Resistance, or the *chasse* (hunt) and the

PROVENCE

FLOYD'S

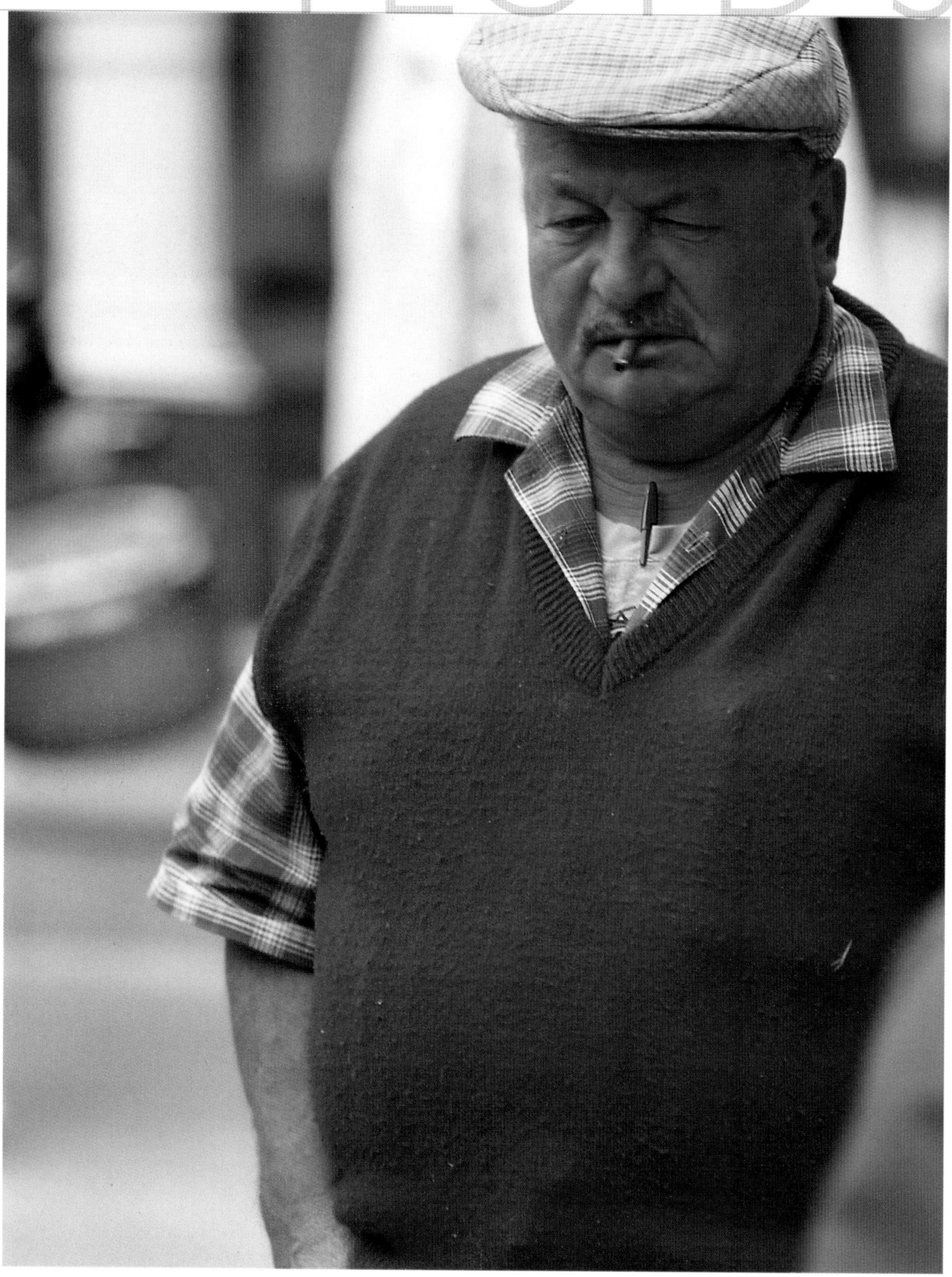

PROVENCE

impending excitement of the autumnal mushroom-gathering season and the mystery and magic of truffles. They will talk about food, such as *tapénade* – a purée of black olives spread on bread, or *soupe au pistou* – a wonderful vegetable soup flavoured with basil, garlic and pine nuts. They will talk about the *Tiercé*, the state-sponsored trotting races, or of the *Lotto*; they will talk of *pissaladière*, a wonderful, small, onion tart topped with anchovy, olives and tomatoes; they will talk of goat's cheeses as hard and shrivelled as lumps of chalk. They will talk of Christmas and of the Christmas Eve supper taken after midnight mass: *brandade de morue*, a delicious purée of salt cod, olive oil and garlic (fasting fish, out of deference to the Catholic faith), followed by *les treize desserts*, thirteen desserts which will include nuts, crystallised fruits, nougat from Montélimar, pure fruit jellies, marrons glacés and sugared almonds from Aix-en-Provence, to represent Christ and his disciples at the Last Supper. They will talk volubly and knowledgeably of visits (in fact quite rare) to the coast – to Sète, or Marseilles or beyond – for a Sunday treat, to eat *bourride*, an exquisite fish stew in a thick, yellow-ochre, creamy garlic sauce – a dish first brought to the French Mediterranean coast by Venetian traders many, many centuries before McDonalds

became the official restaurant to the World Cup in France in 1998. *Comme on dit: la nostalgie n'est plus ce qu'elle était; plus ça change, ça change!*

If you should find yourself in Carcassonne, visit La Barbacane and try the *pissaladière* or the *lotte rôtie* (roast monkfish); the rabbits are not bad, either, by the way. Quail is brilliant in Provence, as is thrush (*grives*) pâté, so if you happen to find yourself in Béziers, go to La Framboisier and try the *salade de caille aux lentilles* (quail salad with lentils). In Aix-en-Provence, at the Clos de la Violette, you will find two refined examples of classic Provençal cuisine: fresh asparagus with truffle ravioli (in the spring only, by the way) and, in the winter, a *pot au feu* of oxtail and truffles. They also have excellent wines from the Coteaux d'Aix-en-Provence. My absolute favourite town is Avignon and my first choice of restaurant is Hiély-Lucullus in the Rue de la République, which, to my certain knowledge, has retained its Michelin star for at least twenty-five years. It has a super sister restaurant which is much cheaper, called La Fourchette, just off the Place de l'Horloge.

PROVENCE

This is a wonderful region, a place – according to Ford Maddox Ford – where the sun always shines and the Brussels sprout would never prosper; but that was many, many years ago. It is now a prestigious wine producing region, also growing olives, cherries, apricots, asparagus and primeur vegetables, including the ubiquitous Brussels sprout and the Golden Delicious apple (yuk!)

Rhône and Provence reds are among my favourite wines and those I tasted were all excellent. Many of the wines are high in fruit and alcohol, with a super taste of blackberries, sunshine, burnt valleys and hot stones. A good little wine is amusingly called Vinsobres, and other fine wines include Côte Rôtie, Hermitage, and the white wines of Condrieu and Château Grillet. All are terrific with cheeses, meats, game and stews. For me the Provence rosés are the tops. They can taste light and dry with a hint of rhubarb. They are very nice, with low acidity. Rosés from the Loire and from (dare I say) Mateus are far too sweet for my taste. But I can drink Provençal rosé till the bourride is cooked and way beyond the aïoli.

In former times the Languedoc region was infamous for producing vast quantities of low quality Vin de Table, that came in those wonderful litre bottles with pop-off plastic stoppers, and which I used to quite like, but now the region has been modernised and varietal wines called simply Sauvignon Blanc, Chardonnay, Pinot Noir or Cabernet Sauvignon are all pretty reliable – good even.

RHÔNE VALLEY

region of Côtes-du-Rhône

Condrieu

Tournon • Tain-l'Hermitage

Valence

Privas • Drôme

ARDÈCHE

NORTHERN RHÔNE
SOUTHERN RHÔNE

Montélimar

COTEAUX DU
TRICASTIN

Nyons

CÔTES - DU - RHÔNE -
VILLAGES

Orange • Châteauneuf-du-Pape

CÔTES - DU -
RHÔNE

Carpentras

Avignon

CÔTES - DU -
VENTOUX

Apt

Rhône

THE RHONE WINE
REGION

RHONE

As we travel south through Burgundy, the climate grows warmer all the time. The watershed between the Atlantic Ocean and the Mediterranean Sea is crossed just north west of Dijon, but somehow the landscape still has a northern feel. It is the city of Lyon, just south of Beaujolais, which feels like the gateway to the south and the inland sea. It is here that the traveller from the north first encounters the River Rhône.

The Rhône starts its life high in the Swiss Alps, where it has a glacier as its source. The river sweeps down the Valais, before halting for a while by forming Lake Geneva. In so doing it makes up part of the stunning view one has from the Swiss vineyards around Lausanne. From Geneva it squeezes its way between the Jura and the Alps, before reaching Lyon and joining the River Saône. It turns to the south, and from there its fate is sealed, flowing directly to its end in the Mediterranean. However, in shaping the landscape along its banks, this final leg of the Rhône's journey has given us one of France's great vineyard regions. It is seen here sweeping through the twin towns of Tournon and Tain l'Hermitage.

The climate in the Rhône valley is fairly warm and dry, which favours the production of red wines. The one peculiarity about the climate is the Mistral. Every so often, this strong cold wind blows down the Rhône from the north. In parts of the valley the vines have to be supported by stakes to protect them from damage. The Mistral, however, can sometimes have a beneficial effect, drying the vines quickly after heavy rain and so protecting them from fungal diseases.

The wines of the Rhône

The precipitous terraced vineyards of the Northern Rhône

The Northern Rhône

The Rhône wine region is divided into two sections. In the northern Rhône the river has carved its way through hard granite. This has created a narrow gorge, on the steep sides of which the best vineyards are planted. In several places this has involved building terraces for the vines. Production in this northern section of the Rhône is small, but the quality can be fantastic.

The only black grape grown in the northern Rhône is the Syrah, capable of producing some very fine red wines (as it does in Australia, where it is known as Shiraz). When young, Syrah wines are deeply coloured, and packed with dark fruit flavours. With age, their bouquet becomes meaty and leathery. Although full bodied in the mouth, top Syrah wines

RHONE

never seem to be as tough and austere as equivalent wines made from Cabernet Sauvignon. Nonetheless, a serious Syrah can keep well for a couple of decades at least.

The two great northern Rhône reds are Côte Rôtie and Hermitage, and the best examples of both come from the sort of steep vineyards described above. The AC Cornas is also capable of producing some very substantial red wines. The international wine buying public has 'discovered' these leading Rhône wines recently, so prices have increased sharply. A couple of other appellations offer good value for money, however, and are worth looking out for: the red wines from Crozes-Hermitage and Saint-Joseph are often peppery and fruity, perhaps lacking the structure and substance of their august neighbours, but they can be very enjoyable nonetheless.

The appellations of Hermitage, Crozes-Hermitage and Saint-Joseph all make small amounts of dry white wine from a pair of grape varieties, the Marsanne and the Roussanne. The real gem amongst the dry white wines of the Rhône Valley, however, is the tiny appellation of Condrieu. Until comparatively recently, AC Condrieu, and its even more microscopic neighbour AC Château Grillet, were the only places on earth to make white wine from the Viognier grape. Condrieu can be a magical wine, rich yet dry on the palate, with a glorious peachy aroma. The rediscovery of this appellation in modern times has led growers around the world to scramble to plant the Viognier, to see if they can capture some of the magic of Condrieu. Viognier wines are now produced in places as far apart as California, Australia and Languedoc.

The Southern Rhône

The southern section of the Rhône wine region looks and feels very different from the north. In the south the river has escaped from the narrow granite gorge, and has spread itself across a huge flattish plain. The soil in many of the vineyards is made up of large pebbles. Instead of small plots of vines on steep terraced slopes, in parts of the southern Rhône one can stand in vineyards and see kilometre after

Grape varieties

MUSCAT (also known as Moscato or Moscatel). This grape is responsible for the production of a number of sweet, often fortified, white wines. Most of the grape-growing countries which border the Mediterranean cultivate Muscat, producing wines such as Moscatel de Valencia, Asti Spumante and Muscat of Samos. The Southern Rhône is home to Muscat de Beaumes de Venise, which is both sweet and fortified. Alsace, by contrast, goes for a dry version of Muscat. When young, Muscat has a pronounced grapey aroma. Older, cask matured, sweet Muscats can develop an intense raisiny richness. Liqueur Muscats are produced in the Rutherglen area of Victoria (Australia).

GRENACHE (known as the Garnacha in Spain). Important but often overlooked, Grenache is the most widely planted black grape variety in the southern Rhône, producing wines high in alcohol and often full of soft, jammy, spicy fruit. It is a component of many of the blends used in the traditional reds from southern France and northern Spain. In Australia it has become fashionable in recent years.

SYRAH (known as Shiraz in Australia). Syrah is the only black grape cultivated in the northern Rhône. In recent years Languedoc-Roussillon has enjoyed a lot of success with this variety, which is also widely planted in Australia. Syrah wines tend to have a very dark colour, aromas of bramble and pepper, and on the palate can be quite chunky and full bodied.

Red Winemaking

Red wine has to be made from black grapes. The red winemaking process starts in the same way as white wine, with the grapes being crushed and, usually, destalked. The crunch difference is that once the black grapes are crushed, the mass of skins, pulp and pips are pumped directly to the fermentation vat. Some winemakers do not even destalk the grapes, so the stalks end up in the vat as well. In the old days the black grapes would have been tipped into open tanks and trodden to achieve the required crushing.

Additions of sugar and of sulphur dioxide can be made to the vat in the same way as for white wine. The fermentation will start, but this time in contact with the black grape skins. The colour from the skins gradually leaches into the fermenting must, along with tannins and flavour. Tannins are dry, astringent-tasting substances found in grape skins (and tea leaves). They give red wines a lot of their 'mouthfeel', and

contribute to their ability to age.

The grape skins tend to float to the top of the fermentation vats (carried there by the carbon dioxide). This is less than ideal and winemakers take various measures to make sure that the fermenting wine mixes with the skins. The two most widespread techniques are *remontage* and *pigeage*. 'Remontage', or 'pumping over', involves draining some wine out of the bottom of the fermentation vat, pumping it up to the top, then spraying it over the skins. This technique has the advantage of aerating the fermenting wine, which helps the yeast to grow. 'Pigeage', or 'punching the cap', is usually achieved by using something that looks like a rowing oar to push the skins down into the fermenting wine.

To further aid the extraction of colour and flavour, red wines tend to be fermented at warmer temperatures than white wines: between 25°C and 30°C is the norm. This means that the fermentation will be faster, often only taking around a week. If a very concentrated, tannic, red wine is required, the skins can be left in the vat after fermentation to

'Pumping over' to mix the fermenting red wine and the skins

allow even more extraction to take place (a process called 'cuvaison').

With the fermentation completed, a valve at the bottom of the vat is opened and most of the red wine runs out. This fraction is called the 'Free Run Wine'. The skins and pips are then emptied out of the vat and put into a press. The wine extracted in this way is called 'Press Wine' and is very dark and tannic. Winemakers tend to keep the Press Wine and the Free Run Wine separate at first, only making a final decision on the blending later on during the maturation.

The new red wine is then encouraged to undergo malolactic fermentation. Whereas some winemakers choose to block this process for certain white wines, the general consensus is that all red wines should have a malolactic fermentation, as its softening effect helps to make the tannins in a red wine seem less harsh.

Once the fermentation stages are completed, the wine can be racked off its lees and begin its maturation.

The classic approach to winemaking outlined above tends to produce red wines with not just a deep colour, but also a backbone of tannin. This is fine if a solid red wine, needing maturation in wood and/or in the bottle, is required. Limiting a wine's *cuvaison* will cut down on the extraction of tannin. However, if a light fruity red wine for drinking young is the objective, then winemakers can employ a technique called 'carbonic maceration'. Whole bunches of black grapes are sealed in a vat and left in an atmosphere of carbon dioxide. In this way a deeply coloured juice can be released from the grapes, accompanied by very little tannin. Beaujolais Nouveau is the most famous wine made this way, but the technique is used elsewhere in France. The drawback of making a wine exclusively by carbonic maceration is that with little tannin the wine will not keep well.

kilometre of vines stretching across the plain. The regimented rows of wire-trained vines, such as one sees in Northern France, are less common in the Southern Rhône. Here, the vines are traditionally bush-trained (see 'Pruning, training and planting density', page 81).

Rather than working only with the Syrah for red wine production, in the southern Rhône a blend of black grapes is employed. The most important of these is the Grenache, often criticised in the past for producing wines that were clumsy – rather high in alcohol, coarse, and not able to age gracefully. Although the true value of Grenache is now better appreciated and it has, indeed, become fashionable in recent years, its past reputation may well account for the use of a blend of grapes by the growers in the southern Rhône. The core quartet consists of Grenache, Cinsault, Mourvèdre and Syrah.

The basic designation for the wines of the Rhône Valley – but in practice only used for those from the south – is AC Côtes du Rhône. Enormous quantities of this generally decent, glugging red wine are produced. Given the size of the appellation, it goes without saying that the quality can be very variable. The AC Côtes du Rhône-Villages works rather like the equivalent appellations in the Mâconnais and Beaujolais. In other words, the better villages in the southern Rhône can use the Côtes du Rhône-Villages appellation for their wines, which will generally have more depth and concentration than a straight Côtes du Rhône.

A number of villages actually have their own appellations. The most famous of these is Châteauneuf-du-Pape. Lying between Orange and Avignon, this substantially sized vineyard area produces heady, alcoholic, spicy red wines. Although Châteauneuf-du-Pape can be very good, rather like its humble neighbour Côtes du Rhône it is prone to variability. The pebbly, 'pudding stone' soil (seen on page 59) which characterises many parts of the southern Rhône is particularly abundant in some parts of Châteauneuf-du-Pape. As well as being good for drainage and low in organic matter, the pudding stones absorb the sun's heat during the day. At night,

the stones radiate heat, a bit like a night storage heater. This extra warmth helps the grapes to ripen faster, giving some very high sugar levels. The resulting high alcohol level in the finished wine (the appellation specifies a minimum of 12.5% ABV) makes Châteauneuf-du-Pape ideal for killing the pain of life on a Friday night.

Generally slightly cheaper than Châteauneuf-du-Pape, but in the same substantial red wine mould, are the appellations of Gigondas, Lirac and Vacqueyras.

Several of the southern Rhône appellations, including Châteauneuf-du-Pape, allow for the production of dry white wines. These have to be made from local white grapes, and while they can be fresh and attractive when young, are not life changing.

Ordinary as its white wines are, the southern Rhône can claim to produce the best rosé in France. AC Tavel is pretty serious for a rosé, often having good depth of flavour and a significant whack of alcohol. It is made in the dry style, and can work well with food.

The southern Rhône is also home to France's most famous fortified wine, Muscat de Beaumes de Venise. This is one of a whole family of sweet fortified wines produced in southern France, generically known as 'Vins Doux Naturels'. These are made by allowing grape must to start fermenting, but then the yeast are killed by adding grape spirit to bump the alcohol level up to 15% ABV. The arresting of the fermentation leaves a lot of unfermented sugar, resulting in wines that can be intensely sweet. Muscat de Beaumes de Venise comes from the village of Beaumes de Venise, and is obviously made from the Muscat grape. The sweetness of the wine has meant that many people automatically think of it as a dessert wine; it is, however, equally pleasant drunk chilled as an aperitif. The nearby village of Rasteau makes another style of Vin Doux Naturel – a sweet, fortified red wine made primarily from Grenache.

Just on the borders of the core southern Rhône vineyards are some minor appellations which make everyday wines very much in the Côtes du Rhône style: Côtes du Ventoux and Coteaux du Tricastin both produce simple quaffing reds.

Who made this wine?

Perverse as it seems, one of the most difficult things to find out about some wines is who actually grew the grapes and made the wine. By law, the only name and address which has to appear on a label is that of the bottler. He may or may not be the grower or the winemaker. Roughly speaking, there are three main ways that wines tend to be produced:

1. The most obvious one is for a grower to grow his own grapes, pick them, ferment and mature the wine, and bottle it on his own premises. In other words, the producer and his team are responsible for everything from the vineyard to the bottle. This approach allows total control, and many of the world's great wines are made this way. French examples are often labelled 'Mis en bouteille au château' or 'Mis en bouteille au domaine'.

2. Owning one's own winery is an expensive business, so in many parts of France the individual growers have a stake in a co-operative winery. They take their grapes to the co-operative winery each autumn, and the winery does the fermentation, maturation and bottling. Many co-operatives subsequently look after the marketing of the wine as well. The individual growers will then receive a dividend based on the quantity and quality of grapes they provided.

3. The other option for a grower without his own winery is to sell his grapes to a commercial winery. Such a winery may be buying grapes from dozens of different growers. Very often such big operations will also buy in finished wine from co-operatives and individual domaines. The French name for such merchants in wine is négociants.

The amazing 'pudding stones' of Châteauneuf-du-Pape

French wine law

The European Union's wine law divides all wines produced in the EU into two families, Table Wines and Quality Wines Produced in a Specified Region (mercifully abbreviated to QWPSR, or VQPRD in French). Each EU country has to use this framework when classifying and labelling its wines. The French classification is as follows:

TABLE WINE

Vin de Table. This is the basic category of French table wine, and can be a blend of wines from anywhere in France. In practice, most *Vin de Table* is produced in Languedoc-Roussillon and other parts of south-western France. No designation of vintage or grape variety can be shown on the label of a *Vin de Table*.

Vin de Pays. The creation of this superior category of table wine has encouraged many growers and consumers to trade up from *Vin de Table*. These 'country wines' come from designated geographical areas, and where relevant can indicate grape variety and vintage on their labels. Like *Vins de Table*, most *Vins de Pays* come from Languedoc-Roussillon; famous areas of production are Gard, Aude, Hérault and Oc.

QUALITY WINE

Vin Délimité de Qualité Supérieure (VDQS). This is the lower level of quality wine in France. The rules are similar to those for *Appellation Contrôlée*, laying down production zones, soil types, permitted grape varieties etc. However, nowadays VDQS tends to be restricted to just a handful of fairly obscure regional wines. There are very few commercially significant VDQS wines left, most of the larger ones having been promoted to AC. Examples sometimes seen on the export market are Sauvignon du Haut Poitou, Cabardès and Côtes de Saint-Mont.

Appellation Contrôlée (AC), or more correctly *Appellation d'Origine Contrôlée* (AOC). This is the top designation for a French wine. The most important thing an AC does is to define precisely where a wine can come from. So, for instance, Appellation Gevrey-Chambertin Contrôlée can only come from the village of Gevrey-Chambertin. The rules then go on to specify which types of soils and grapes are allowed. Maximum yields (to prevent over-cropping) and minimum alcohol levels (to ensure decent ripeness) are also laid down. In some cases there are rules about how the wine should be fermented and matured. However, *Appellation Contrôlée* does have its limitations. There are wines which comply with the rules, but which are still pretty dull. As with most products, the ultimate responsibility for quality lies with the producer.

RHONE

WINE TASTING NOTES

CROZES-HERMITAGE

Pedley "Deep, dark, ruby body. Mid ruby rim. Dark, spicy, peppery, leathery nose. Quite heavy, with some stewed berry, damson and prune character. Dry, mid-low acidity, highish alcohol. A moderate level of tannin. Quite chewy and full in the mouth. Good, dry and savoury length."

CHATEAUNEUF-DU-PAPE

Pedley "Deepish garnet body. Broad garnet rim. Quite lush and floral at first on the nose. Very ripe, jammy fruit. Spicy and herbal, with hints of dark chocolate. The alcohol comes through. Dry and smooth, low acidity, very warm alcohol. Moderate to soft tannins. Round and lush. Full bodied. Quite a long, peppery finish."

COTES DU RHONE-VILLAGES

Pedley "Fairly deep crimson body. Mid pink rim. Very soft, broad, open, loganberry and fig fruit. Some spice as well. Inky. Dry, low acidity, warm alcohol. Soft and round tannins. Mid-bodied. Very appealing. Mid length of finish."

MUSCAT DE BEAUMES DE VENISE

Pedley "Mid straw colour. Very viscous appearance. Very intense, perfumed, fragrant nose. Grapey and scented. Some alcohol apparent as well. Very sweet on the palate, lowish acidity, very marked alcohol. Heavy and sticky. Lots of white fruit flavours. Mid length of finish."

Floyd food notes

approximately 1.25 kg/2 lb 12 oz thick fillet of salt cod

3 dozen tinned snails (without shells)

FOR THE STOCK:

1.5 litres/2¾ pints water

1 carrot, peeled and chopped

1 onion, peeled and stuck with cloves

1 small leek, trimmed and chopped

3 or 4 garlic cloves, crushed but not peeled

1 bouquet garni of fresh parsley, thyme, bayleaf and celery leaves

salt and pepper

FOR THE AIOLI:

8 garlic cloves

2 egg yolks

approximately 450 ml/15 fl oz extra virgin olive oil

juice of 1 lemon

salt and pepper

FOR THE GARNISH:

1 kg/2lb 4 oz new potatoes, scraped or peeled

1 kg/2 lb 4 oz small white onions, peeled

Le grand aïoli
(Platter of salt cod, snails, eggs and vegetables served with garlic mayonnaise)

Serves 6

The traditional, festive summer dish of my Provence, eaten communally. This is a generous platter of salt cod, snails, boiled potatoes, carrots, artichokes, green beans and hardboiled eggs, accompanied by a bowlful of thick yellow garlicky mayonnaise. Back home in Britain, you will probably have to make do with tinned snails for your platter. This is fine, as long as you rinse them thoroughly.

The day before making the dish, soak the salt cod in several changes of fresh, cold water. Leave to soak overnight, then rinse thoroughly. The snails will also need to be very well rinsed before cooking.

To make the stock, place all the ingredients in a large pot, bring to the boil and simmer for 40–50 minutes. Set aside.

For the *aïoli* sauce, crush the garlic using a mortar and pestle, then whisk in the egg yolks. Drizzle in the olive oil, stirring or whisking constantly, until you have a thick yellow mayonnaise. Stir in the lemon juice and add salt and pepper to taste. Alternatively, crush the garlic in a garlic press, then put all the ingredients except the olive oil into a food processor or liquidiser. Turn on the motor and process for a few seconds before drizzling in the oil with the motor running, until you achieve the same yellow mayonnaise.

Next, prepare the vegetables for the garnish. The artichokes will need to have their stems snapped off, and the pointed top removed by slicing with a sharp knife, about one third of the way down and parallel with the base. Spread open the central leaves and remove the furry choke – a melon-baller helps with this. Trim off any spiky leaf-tips and rub all cut surfaces with a slice of lemon. Cook in boiling, salted water until you can easily pull one of the fleshy leaves away from the base, then drain upside down.

600 g/1 lb 5 oz young, small carrots, scraped

600 g/1 lb 5 oz green haricot beans, topped and tailed

1 small cauliflower, trimmed

6 small courgettes, trimmed

6 small artichokes (see method for preparation)

6 hard-boiled eggs, halved

salt and pepper

Cook all the remaining vegetables individually in boiling, salted water – the potatoes should be tender, the rest *al dente*. Drain well and keep the vegetables warm.

Strain enough of the reserved stock into a saucepan to cover the cod fillet. Poach the cod gently for about 10 minutes. Check that the fish is almost cooked and add the snails for a further 10 minutes. Drain thoroughly. Now arrange the fish, the snails, the vegetables and the eggs on a huge serving platter, in an elegant but boldly rustic manner. Serve the *aïoli* in a separate bowl.

Recommended wine –
white Crozes-Hermitage

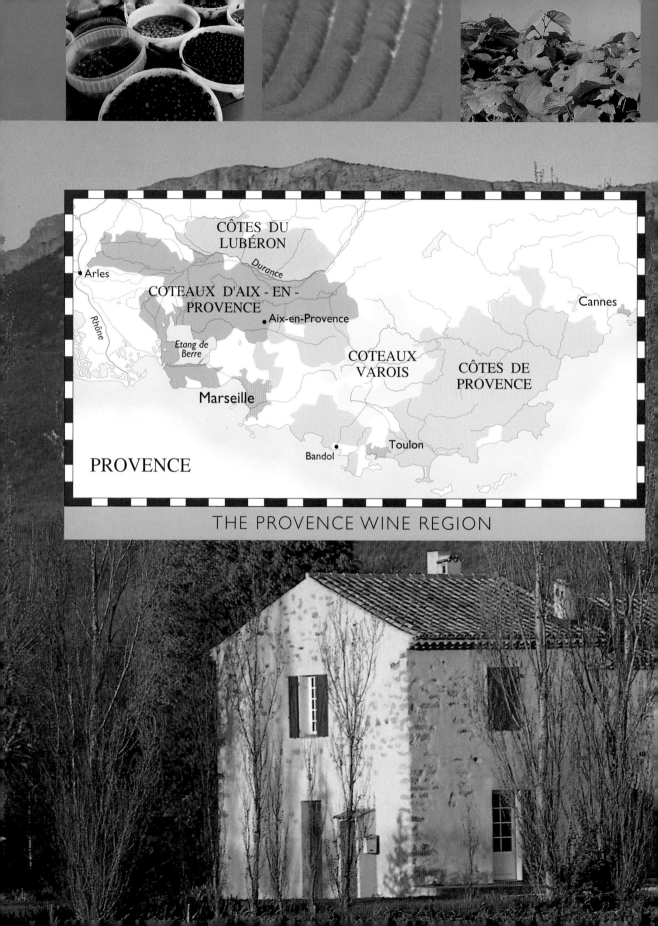

CÔTES DU
LUBÉRON

Durance

Arles

COTEAUX D'AIX - EN -
PROVENCE
Aix-en-Provence

Rhône

*Etang de
Berre*

COTEAUX
VAROIS

CÔTES DE
PROVENCE

Cannes

Marseille

Toulon

PROVENCE

Bandol

THE PROVENCE WINE REGION

PROVENCE

*A*s a region, Provence summons up several contrasting images. The paintings of Cézanne capture the distinctive stark beauty of the country-side around Aix-en-Provence and St-Maximin la Ste-Beaune (seen here). Writers and film makers have often depicted this inland Provence as an Arcadia. It is still very beautiful, and is certainly much wealthier than it was even a generation ago. Down on the coast are the sophisticated resorts, reaching their apogee in Monaco. And then there is the urban squalor, and poisonous racism. All are part of the reality of Provence.

Provence enjoys the classic Mediterranean climate, with a mild, wet winter and a hot, dry summer. In fact, so mild is the winter than vines will sometimes start to bud in January. However, there is more vintage variation than one might expect, with drought and storms capable of upsetting the ripening of the grapes.

Provence is primarily a producer of decent, moderately priced, everyday wines. Its dry rosé, often encountered in the curvaceous *flûte à corset* bottle, is perhaps the best known style. When young and fresh, and served well chilled, it is the perfect informal summer wine. The production of dry white wines is fairly small, and like the rosés they are generally simple wines. Where Provence deserves more serious attention is for its reds. That said, many are merely light and fruity, but a number are more substantial and structured.

The wines of Provence

Most of the vineyards in the region are covered by three appellations: Côtes de Provence, Coteaux Varois and Coteaux d'Aix-en-Provence. Together, these three areas run from just outside Cannes in the east to Arles in the west. The black grape varieties grown in these areas are mainly those we are familiar with from the Rhône, in other words Grenache, Mourvèdre and Syrah. One or two local varieties are also allowed, as is the Cabernet Sauvignon. The increased planting of the latter is seen as one element in the much improved quality of the region's red wines. Permitted white grapes include Clairette, Ugni Blanc, Grenache Blanc and Vermentino.

If Provence has a great traditional wine area, then it is AC Bandol. Lying just to the west of Toulon, this small appellation covers dry whites, rosés and reds. It is the powerful, chunky reds that are the basis of the area's claim to fame. The key black grape is the Mourvèdre, backed up by the usual line-up: Grenache, Cinsault, Syrah and Carignan.

Other tiny local appellations include Cassis, Palette and Bellet, whose wines are rarely seen on the export market. One that is seen overseas occasionally is Côtes du Lubéron. This area lies north of Aix-en-Provence, on the borders of the southern Rhône region (it is often included in the latter). Reds, rosés and dry whites are produced, based on the usual southern Rhône/Provence grape mix. The wines are generally fruity, pleasant, and not too expensive.

(left) The house in Provence we all dream of

(right) There aren't many people in France making wine this way any more!

Rosé winemaking

The obvious way to make a rosé wine would be to blend some red wine with some white. Strangely, this approach is rarely used (though Rosé Champagne is often made this way). The more normal technique is to start with black grapes, and crush them gently. The juice from these crushed grapes is left with the skins for a period of time between six and forty-eight hours.

In this time, a small amount of colour leaks from the skins into the juice, turning it pink. Once enough pink colour has been extracted, the juice is drained off. It is then treated as if it were a white wine, being fermented cool, and receiving little if any maturation before bottling. In addition to serving them chilled, it is worth remembering that rosé wines are generally best drunk young.

The Vine

VINE AGE

The age of a vine has a big effect on the quality and quantity of fruit produced, and therefore also on the cost of the resulting wine.

When a 'baby' vine arrives from the nursery and is planted out it is very small. After planting, all that is visible is a twig sticking a few centimetres out of the soil. It will not be productive for some time, often three to four years. This is one reason why starting a vineyard from scratch is such an expensive business.

Once productive, the young vine will give a generous yield. But at this stage the concentration of flavour in the grapes is not great, and the resulting wine quality is ordinary. However, as the vine ages, the size of its crop decreases, but the quality of its fruit increases. Growers differ somewhat on what they describe as 'old vines', but over thirty years old is a reasonable guideline. Some vineyards, however, contain vines that are over a hundred years old. These veterans are obviously only producing a few bunches of grapes, but they are treasured for their quality.

Many of the world's great wines are made from the fruit of old vines. But with low yields, such wines are always going to be expensive. Occasionally, growers in France who are using grapes from old vines will print the words 'Vieilles Vignes' on the label.

Everyday wines obviously cannot afford the luxury of low yielding old vines. What is more, some old vineyards can be very diseased, and so many growers replant on a regular basis to maintain production levels.

PHYLLOXERA AND GRAFTING

As well as being at the mercy of the weather, the vine is at risk from fungal diseases, and prey to various pests. Most can be dealt with effectively (rabbits, for instance, end up in the cooking pot). The most significant pest of the vine is a tiny louse with a terrifying name, Phylloxera vastatrix. Phylloxera spends much of its life underground, where it feeds on the roots of the vine. In the case of *Vitis vinifera* (the European vine), the roots cannot heal themselves after being attacked and the vine will die. This louse got out into most of the world's vineyards in the second half of the nineteenth century, and caused massive devastation. Conventional sprays were next to

(right) Bench grafted Chardonnay vines

useless against this underground-dweller. Fortunately, it was observed that although the European vine was destroyed by Phylloxera, the American vine species could heal their roots and so tolerate the pest.

One solution might have been to replant the world's vineyards with American vines. However, the quality of wine produced by native American vines is pretty ordinary. A better solution is to plant an American vine and then graft a cutting of a European vine on to this American rootstock. This way, everything below the soil is American vine, and Phylloxera-resistant, whereas everything above the ground is European vine, capable of giving us quality fruit. Nowadays, much of the actual grafting is done in the nursery, a process called 'bench grafting'. Most of the world's vineyards are now planted with grafted vines.

Cleaning up wine

Once a wine has completed its maturation, it is necessary to clean it up in preparation for bottling. This may entail fining, cold treatment and filtration.

Even after fairly long maturation, when the wine will have had ample opportunity to settle out any suspended material, it may still have a haze. This can be removed by fining. The fining agent is added to the wine whilst it is still in cask or vat. Over a period of days the fining agent sinks down through the wine, picking up the haze material, and forming a sediment at the bottom of the storage vessel. The clarified wine can then be racked off. The main fining agent for white wine is a special clay called bentonite. Red wine, by contrast, is traditionally fined with beaten egg whites.

Another potential problem involves tartaric acid, the main acid in most grapes. This acid provides the freshness in wine which is so important to its overall balance. However, occasionally some of the tartaric acid can precipitate in the bottle, forming tartrate crystals. These crystals are totally harmless, and the quality of the wine is unaffected. Careful decanting can remove them. However, because they are unsightly, and because of consumer resistance, many producers try to avoid the risk of tartrate crystals forming in the bottle. This can be achieved by putting the wine into a vat and chilling it to around minus 3°C for a week, during which time any excess tartrate should crystallise out. The wine can then be drained off. Even after cold treatment, however, some wines can still throw a tartrate deposit.

The final treatments involve making sure there are no remaining yeast or bacteria in the wine. By spinning a wine at high speed in a centrifuge, most of the yeast can be removed.

However, to be absolutely sure all the microbes are removed, most wines undergo filtration before bottling. There are various grades of filter: Kieselguhr (a type of earth) is used when a wine is still quite cloudy, cellulose filter pads give a finer degree of filtration, and if the winemaker wants to be absolutely sure no yeast or bacteria get through to the bottle then a membrane filter will be used.

It is worth sounding a note of caution about all these cleaning up processes. If a wine went through all of the above – fining, cold treatment, centrifugation and three types of filter – it would certainly be stable and clear. However, there would not be much flavour left either! The great skill is to do as little as possible to the wine, whilst ensuring that there are no problems once it is bottled.

WINE TASTING NOTES

COTEAUX D'AIX-EN-PROVENCE ROSE

Pedley "Pale, orangey pink. Lightish aroma, but ripe and juicy nonetheless. Hints of strawberry jam and banana. Round. Dry, moderate acidity and moderate alcohol. Light bodied. Simple fruitiness. Fairly short finish."

COTES DU LUBERON

Pedley "Mid intensity of cherry-red body. Fairly broad pink rim. Soft, but with lots of immediate, ripe red fruits on the nose. Raspberry jam. Slightly herbal. Dry, lowish acidity, moderate alcohol. Fairly light bodied, with light soft tannins as well. Very open fruit character. Mid to short finish."

BANDOL

Pedley "Deepish ruby-pink body. Mid pink rim. Very powerful, super ripe cherries, spicy, peppery nose. Figs and bakewell tart. Dry, lowish acidity, mid-high alcohol. Mid-bodied, but with intense spicy fruit coming through. Underpinned by an austere grip of sandy tannins. Savoury and uncompromising on the finish."

Floyd food notes

FOR THE AIOLI:

8 garlic cloves

2 egg yolks

approximately 450 ml/15 fl oz extra virgin olive oil

juice of 1 lemon

salt and pepper

FOR THE BOURRIDE:

a couple of leeks

a couple of carrots

a couple of onions

a stick of celery

extra virgin olive oil

4 live lobsters or crayfish

1 bottle dry white wine

8 thick fillets of assorted, firm-fleshed fish (bass, monkfish, red mullet, etc.)

600 ml/1 pint of double cream

a good packet of saffron strands

salt and pepper

1 tin or tube of harissa (Moroccan chilli paste)

boiled potatoes

Recommended wine – Coteaux d'Aix-en-Provence Rosé

Bourride
(Garlic-sauced seafood stew)

Serves 4-8

You can make the aïoli well in advance of serving, put it into a plastic container and leave it in the fridge while you shop for the remaining ingredients. The crayfish you can use as an alternative to lobster are also sold as crawfish, or spiny lobster; they are big, reddish brown creatures and have nothing to do with the little freshwater shellfish. A white Châteauneuf-du-Pape would be ideal to use in this dish.

First make a jolly good dollop of *aïoli*. To do this, crush the garlic using a mortar and pestle, then whisk in the egg yolks. Drizzle in the olive oil, stirring or whisking constantly, until you have a thick yellow mayonnaise. Stir in the lemon juice and add salt and pepper to taste. Alternatively, crush the garlic in a garlic press, then put all the ingredients except the olive oil into a food processor or liquidiser. Turn on the motor and process for a few seconds before drizzling in the oil with the motor running, until you achieve the same yellow mayonnaise. Store, covered, in the fridge until required.

Chop the vegetables finely; there should be enough to cover the bottom of a large pan in which you will poach the lobsters. Pour some olive oil into the pan and soften the vegetables. Then pop in the lobsters or crayfish, cover them with a mixture of white wine and water, add some salt and pepper, and bring to the boil. The moment the liquid has boiled, turn off the heat, clamp a lid onto the pan and leave the lobsters to cook in the residual heat for twenty minutes. Remove the lobsters, turn on the heat under the lobster-flavoured stock and poach the fillets of fish gently (don't boil them). While the fillets are poaching, cut the lobsters in half, place these on a platter and keep them warm. As soon as the fish is ready, lift the fillets from the pot, place them alongside the lobster halves and keep both fish and lobster warm.

Now strain the poaching liquid and discard the vegetables and half of the stock. Over a fierce flame, reduce the rest to a third of its volume. Lower the heat and whisk in the cream and saffron. You should begin to get a custard-like consistency. Finally, whisk in two thirds of your *aïoli* until you have a thick, creamy garlicky sauce. Strain this sauce over the fish and lobster. The remainder of the *aïoli* can be spooned over the top of the dish. Oh and the harissa, I hear you cry. Fry some little croutons of bread in olive oil, spread the spicy concoction on the croutons and float them in the sauce. Serve with boiled potatoes.

St Chinian

Faugères

FAUGÈRES

COTEAUX DU
LANGUEDOC

Carcassonne

MINERVOIS

ST-CHINIAN

Limoux

Béziers

MUSCAT DE
FRONTIGNAN

Montpellier

BLANQUETTE
DE LIMOUX

Quillan

CORBIÈRES

Narbonne

Frontignan

FITOU

CÔTES DU
ROUSSILLON-
VILLAGES

Maury

Fitou

GOLFE   DU   LION

Rivesaltes

MUSCAT DE RIVESALTES

Perpignan

CÔTES
DU
ROUSSILLON

Banyuls

FRANCE
SPAIN

BANYULS

LANGUEDOC AND ROUSSILLON

RHONE

THE LANGUEDOC-ROUSSILLON WINE REGION

LANGUEDOC-ROUSSILLON

Languedoc-Roussillon is the largest vineyard region in France. It starts where the Rhône joins the Mediterranean, and then curves down to the Pyrenées and the border with Spain, sharing with Provence and the southern Rhône the kudos of being the oldest vineyard zone in France. The wealth of the region in Roman times is apparent in the extraordinary surviving monuments, such as the Pont du Gard (pictured on page 77), and the Maison Carrée in Nîmes. The planting of the first vineyards, however, probably significantly predates Roman expansion, and may well have been carried out by the Phoenicians or Ancient Greeks. In the middle ages Languedoc-Roussillon went through turbulent times. Even today the landscape is scattered with fortresses, but none can compare with the massive walled Cité of Carcassonne (seen here).

Although Languedoc-Roussillon could have some pride in the size of its production, it has to be said that until about twenty years ago most of the wine made there was pretty grim. This was not because of any inherent problem with grape growing in the region – two and a half thousand years of vine cultivation should have exposed any flaws along the way. Rather, the problem was more to do with the role that Languedoc-Roussillon found itself fulfilling.

The Mediterranean climate in Languedoc-Roussillon makes wine production a reasonably dependable business. However, until the second half of the last century, the region was quite remote from Paris and the industrial north of France. A lot of the capital's everyday wines used to come from vineyards fairly close to Paris, such as those around Orléans. The arrival of the Phylloxera louse, however, destroyed many of these northern vineyards. By this time, the railway linking the Mediterranean coast with Paris was open. Although Languedoc-Roussillon was also affected by Phylloxera, commercially it made more sense to replant here in the south, now that transport links were so much better. Consequently Languedoc-Roussillon became the country's main source of basic, cheap, commodity wine.

The wines of Languedoc-Roussillon

Table wines

To this day, most of France's Vin de Table comes from Languedoc-Roussillon. The flat high-yielding vineyards, just inland from the coast in Languedoc, are traditionally planted with varieties like Aramon and Alicante Bouschet, specifically to churn out huge volumes of 'vin rouge'. This made sense while there was a huge demand in France for such simple wine. However, wine consumption in France began to fall sharply in modern times, as the trend moved towards drinking less but better. This left the growers in Languedoc spewing out massive volumes of wine for which there was no market – the origin of the 'wine lake', most of which was distilled and sold off for a pittance.

Clearly action had to be taken by the growers, the French government and the authorities in Brussels. A system of grants was set up to encourage

LANGUEDOC-
ROUSSILLON

The Pont du Gard near Nîmes – a stunning example of Roman engineering

growers to grub up vineyards. However, a more positive option was opened for those growers interested in trading up. An upmarket category of table wine was created, called Vin de Pays (see French wine law, page 60). It is probably not too much of an exaggeration to say that the Vin de Pays designation has saved Languedoc from terminal decline, and indeed has allowed the area to turn itself into what many people feel is France's most dynamic vineyard region.

Whilst the rules for Vin de Pays are not as strict as those for VDQS or AC, they do lay down specific production areas and minimum alcohol levels. Vins de Pays are allowed to show their vintage on the label, and can indicate their grape variety(ies) as well. This latter point has been very important, given the boom in varietal wines. The list of permitted varieties which

can be used to make a Vin de Pays is generally much longer than that permitted for a local *Appellation Contrôlée* wine. For instance, traditionally the Viognier grape only grew in the northern Rhône. Now, because it is a permitted variety for Vin de Pays d'Oc, we are seeing much more Viognier successfully grown in Languedoc. In fact, virtually all the classic grapes feature as Vin de Pays varietal wines, with Chardonnay inevitably becoming ubiquitous.

There are well over a hundred Vin de Pays areas in France, many of them in Languedoc-Roussillon. They come in what might be termed three sizes. The regional Vins de Pays cover huge swathes of land. The most famous of these is the Vin de Pays d'Oc which covers the whole of Languedoc-Roussillon. The next size down covers a single *département* (rather like a county). The four found in Languedoc-Roussillon are the Vins de Pays du Gard, de l'Hérault, de l'Aude and des Pyrénées-Orientales. There are then zonal Vins de Pays, which cover small areas within a *département*. For instance, the Vin de Pays des Côtes de Thongue lies in the Hérault *département*, just outside the city of Béziers.

The flexibility inherent in the Vin de Pays category, the right to plant fashionable grapes, and a realisation that old ways had to change, have all contributed to the turn around in fortunes of Languedoc-Roussillon. Innovative local producers have been joined by winemakers from overseas in creating a whole new generation of wines in the region.

Quality wines

Table wines apart, Languedoc-Roussillon has always made a number of decent, rustic reds. The quality of these wines has improved over the years, and most have now achieved *Appellation Contrôlée* status: Corbières, Minervois and Fitou are perhaps best known, but Costières du Nîmes, Coteaux du Languedoc, Saint-Chinian, Faugères and Côtes du Roussillon are all capable of producing worthy wines. The grape mix is very similar to that found in the southern Rhône and

Provence: Carignan, Cinsault, Grenache, Mourvèdre and Syrah. Several of these appellations also allow for the production of rosés and dry white wines, the latter based on a blend of local white grapes such as Bourboulenc, Grenache Blanc and Macabeu.

Languedoc-Roussillon is also a great region for the production of Vins Doux Naturels (fortified sweet wines), a fact often forgotten nowadays. As in the southern Rhône, the white versions are based on Muscat and include AC Muscat de Rivesaltes and AC Muscat de Frontignan. The red versions are based on Grenache, the most famous being AC Banyuls.

It is one of those French oddities that in the midst of this region, which makes so much simple red wine and some fortified sweet wine, a town should be found whose speciality is sparkling white wine. Although the wine producers of Limoux now make still wines as well, the town claims to have been making sparkling wine well before Champagne. Most sparkling Limoux is made by the traditional method in the same way as Champagne. The AC Blanquette de Limoux is based on the local Mauzac grape, while the more recent designation, AC Crémant de Limoux, allows growers to use a significant proportion of Chardonnay and Chenin Blanc in their blends.

Organic wine

Confronted with the pests and diseases that can attack a vine, it is little surprise that most grape growers use a number of sprays and treatments to protect their vines. Herbicides are often used to control weed growth between the vines, and fertilisers are often added to supplement the soil's natural nutrient content. Strict controls on the use of pesticides should mean that residues never find their way into the bottle.

However, there has been a growing realisation that heavyweight use of agrochemicals may not be the answer to all the grape grower's problems. In fact, there is an increasing feeling that such chemicals may be doing serious long-term harm. Firstly, many of the vine's pests and diseases are becoming resistant to insecticides and fungicides. Secondly, the persistent use of herbicides and artificial fertilisers gradually destroys the natural life of the soil, altering its structure. Such a change strikes at the very heart of the belief that the soil contributes to a wine's identity and quality.

An increasing number of growers are cutting back on artificial treatments in the vineyard. Spraying is being limited, and there is a return to the use of compost and manure instead of chemical fertilisers. Natural predators are encouraged to control some of the pests. Ploughing and cover crops are used instead of herbicides. This organic viticulture has quite a following, even amongst the top estates in France. There is an even more radical approach based on the principles of bio-dynamism. This system involves co-ordinating the various cultivation activities with the phases of the moon and stars. Unfortunately, a lack of consensus on permitted practices and sprays means that accreditation is as coherent as that of heavy-weight boxing championships.

Proponents of the organic and bio-dynamic schools of grape growing would argue that their wines actually taste better. Certainly some of the best wines I have tasted in recent years were organically or bio-dynamically produced. Whether this was a direct result of the methods employed is hard to say. Certainly, with our growing concern for the environment, any approach which cuts down on possibly damaging practices is worth exploring.

Pruning, training and planting density

The vine is a vigorous plant, so pruning and training are crucial for keeping it under control. By pruning back in the winter, the grower is reducing the number of buds which will open in the spring. Fewer buds means fewer flowers, and therefore a reduced crop. The hope of course is that the vine's energy will be channelled into the smaller crop, giving better quality of fruit and producing a wine with complexity and depth.

The vines must be trained in order to make the day to day care of the vineyard easier. One of the most popular training systems used in France involves tying one or two of the vine's canes along a wire after pruning. The shoots produced by the cane(s) can then be secured to another higher wire in the spring time. This system, called 'Guyot', creates the neat, hedge-like rows of vines that one often sees in Bordeaux and Burgundy. If the vine's shoots are tied to a post, rather than to a wire, the vine will be roughly goblet shaped, and hence this system is called 'Gobelet' in France. Beaujolais

Dense vine planting in Burgundy

is probably the most famous area to use this type of training. If the vine is pruned back fairly close to its stump, and then the shoots are not supported, one has a bush vine. Most of the vines grown in the southern Rhône are treated like this.

After a visit to one of the New World vineyard areas, it is a shock to come back to France and see how densely the vines are planted in places like Burgundy. The philosophy in France is that competition amongst the closely packed vines is another way of limiting yield and so guaranteeing quality. Of course the big disadvantage is that densely planted vines are hard to cultivate. Specially built 'tractors on stilts' have to be used to straddle the vine rows.

(left) The painstaking pruning of the vines takes place in the winter months

Reading wine labels

To many a wine drinker, it must seem as if quite a few wine labels are designed to create maximum confusion, rather than to encourage you to try the wine. At one extreme you get labels cluttered with irrelevant information, and at the other are some minimalist offerings. In fact, what you can and cannot put on a wine label is very strictly controlled by law. Unfortunately, different countries have different rules about labelling, so a label that is permitted in the USA may be illegal in Canada. As far as France is concerned, membership of the European Union means that its wines fit into EU labelling regulations.

As is so often the case with wine, once you know what is going on things tend to be much less intimidating. So it is with EU wine label rules. These rules specify two types of wine label information; those pieces which are mandatory, and those which are optional.

The optional wine label information includes:
1. The vintage date
2. The grape variety(ies)
3. The colour of the wine
4. The style of the wine: dry, medium or sweet
5. Awards achieved by the wine
6. Serving suggestions

It is one of the ironies of **EU** wine label law that some of the most useful information is purely optional. Mind you, if a Châteauneuf-du-Pape printed all thirteen permitted grapes on its label there would be little room for anything else!

The mandatory wine label information is shown below. Additionally, the lot number must be shown. This does not have to appear on the label itself, just somewhere on the bottle. Some producers print the lot number on the capsule, others on the bottle itself.

The wine's quality status. In France this means a statement as to whether the wine is **Vin de Table, Vin de Pays, VDQS or AC.**

Liquid volume. In other words, how much booze is in the bottle

Percentage alcohol by volume (%**ABV**)

The bottler's name and address

Country of origin

Wine Faults

Various things can go wrong with wine in the winery and during shipping and storage; in fact not until despatched down your throat is the wine completely safe. Modern technology, skilled winemaking, and strict quality control and quality assurance mean that faulty wines are fairly rare. However, you may come across the odd out-of-condition wine from time to time, so it does no harm to know about the sorts of things which can happen.

1. Oxidation. This is one of the more frequent problems. If too much air comes into contact with the wine, at any stage from winery to glass, the wine can oxidise. It loses its aroma, the smell becoming dull and flat, and somewhat reminiscent of sherry. With white wine the wine darkens in colour, and can become quite brown. A whole batch of wine can oxidise, or sometimes just one bottle if a poor cork has let air in.

2. Re-fermentation. This is rare nowadays because most wines are sterile-filtered before bottling. If rogue yeast are not removed from a medium or a sweet wine before bottling, they can start the wine fermenting again. The yeast make the wine cloudy and fizzy. Occasionally the bottle can explode.

3. Volatility. Like re-fermentation, mercifully quite rare nowadays. If rogue bacteria, rather than rogue yeast, attack a wine they can produce acetic acid, turning the wine to vinegar. In fact, wines with this fault do not just smell of vinegar, they can take on a bizarre smell reminiscent of nail varnish remover. Such wines are only of use to solvent abusers.

4. Cork taint. This is alarmingly common and is quite a worry for a lot of producers (see 'Bottling', page 114).

5. Tartrate crystals. As discussed in 'Cleaning up wine', page 70, tartrate crystals are not a fault, but can make a wine seem unsightly.

6. Foreign bodies. The odd fly and spider still die a glorious death in bottles of wine. Shards of glass are occasionally found in wine through problems in manufacture or bottling.

This list of problems might be enough to put the squeamish off wine drinking altogether. Most of the faults are rare, however, and the majority, whilst ruining the wine, do not pose a threat to human health.

LANGUEDOC-ROUSSILLON

FLOYD UNCORKED

WINE TASTING NOTES

VIN DE PAYS D'OC VIOGNIER

Floyd "This was undoubtedly one of the finds of the trip, and in my view leaves a lot of Chablis for dead. It was smooth and lemony, and slightly buttery. An extremely refreshing drink. We finished a couple of bottles with a warm salad of freshly boiled new potatoes and green beans drenched in extra virgin olive oil with chopped basil, mint and sea salt and, my goodness, didn't they all go well together."

Pedley "Deepish straw appearance. Fairly full, ripe and direct on the nose. Apricots, yellow plums and custard. Soft and oily. Dry, mid-high acidity, moderate alcohol. Zingy and fresh on the palate, but with some weight. Moderate length."

MINERVOIS

Floyd "I don't know if this was Bulls Blood or not. It was dark as ink and had a good, soft taste of blackcurrants and chalk. A great winter wine for stews, with little acid and medium alcohol so you can drink lots of it."

Pedley "Dark ruby body. Narrowish purple-pink rim. Some ripe, dark fruit aromas on the nose. Brambles and tar. Plum skins. Dry, lowish acidity, moderate alcohol. A touch of dry, sandy tannin. Mid bodied. A bit dry and meaty on the finish."

COTES DU ROUSSILLON BLANC

Pedley "Pale lemon colour. Simple, clean nose. Just a hint of sappy fruit, but very light. Vaguely oily. Dry, lowish acidity, moderate alcohol. Very light bodied. A touch of pears on the palate. Short but correct on the finish."

VIN DE TABLE ROUGE

Pedley "Fairly pale ruby body. Broad rim. Restrained but correct nose. Some berry fruit. Slightly earthy. Dry, lowish acidity, moderate alcohol. Some dry, rustic tannins. Soft and open on the palate. Short finish."

Floyd food notes

Brandade
(Purée of salt cod)

Serves 4 as a main course, 8 as a starter

This traditional Christmas Eve supper dish – a delicious purée of salt cod, olive oil and garlic – makes for an excellent lunch at any time of the year (salt cod is a year-round standby), and could equally well be served as a starter.

800 g/1 lb 12 oz thick fillet of salt cod

300–400 ml/10–14 fl oz extra virgin olive oil

approximately 25 ml/1 fl oz milk

6 garlic cloves, peeled

grated nutmeg

juice of one lemon

FOR THE ACCOMPANIMENT:

Thin slices of country bread, fried in olive oil

Recommended wine – Viognier

The day before preparing the *brandade*, soak the salt cod in several changes of fresh, cold water and leave to soak overnight. The next day, rinse the fish and cut it into two or three pieces. Place the cod in a saucepan, cover with fresh water and bring gently to the boil. Simmer until cooked, then drain and flake the fish, discarding the skin and the bones. Keep the fish warm.

In two separate small saucepans, warm the olive oil and heat the milk with the garlic cloves. Once the milk is hot, fish out the garlic cloves, and purée together with the cod until you have a thick paste. You are supposed to put the cod and garlic into a mortar and pound it with the pestle, then carry on pounding gently while you alternately add the milk and the oil, then the milk etc., etc., until you have a fairly smooth and fairly thick and creamy fish paste. It is, however, easier to use a small hand held electric liquidiser to first purée the fish and the garlic, then beat in the oil and the hot milk alternately. You should end up with a mixture that resembles puréed potatoes. Season to taste with nutmeg and lemon juice. Serve dollops of the *brandade* on pieces of the fried bread.

Cassoulet

(Stew of beans with pork, sausages and preserved goose)

1 kg/2 lb 4 oz smoked belly of pork, cut into large cubes

100 g/3½ oz goose fat

750 g/1 lb 10 oz dried white haricot beans, soaked in water overnight

6 tomatoes, peeled, deseeded and chopped

2 tablespoons tomato purée

10 garlic cloves

2 bayleaves

1 sprig of thyme

a pinch of powdered cloves

half a litre/18 fl oz of white Languedoc wine and water, mixed

6 pieces of preserved goose or duck

6 Toulouse sausages

6 uncooked garlic sausages

salt and pepper

Serves at least 6

The preserved goose or duck is sold in tins or jars as confit d'oie *or de* canard; *you should find there is plenty of spare fat in the confit tin for use in the recipe, but you can also buy goose fat (graisse d'oie) tinned separately. Some people like to cover the top of the stew with fresh breadcrumbs mixed with chopped parsley and garlic, and grill or gratin until a herby crust is formed.*

Fry the cubes of pork in some of the goose fat in a large casserole until golden. Add the haricot beans, the tomatoes and tomato purée, garlic, herbs, cloves, salt and pepper. Cover with the mixture of wine and water and bring to the boil, then simmer gently for about 1½ hours.

Meanwhile, brown and part cook the sausages in the remaining goose fat and put them, along with the preserved goose or duck pieces, into a greased earthenware casserole. When the beans have almost finished cooking, tip them over the sausages and goose. If necessary add a little more liquid – the consistency should be roughly that of a tin of baked beans – and place in a hot oven (230°C/450°F/Gas Mark 8) for 20–30 minutes, until the confit has heated through and the sausages are cooked. Ideally the whole dish should be cooked in the oven from start to finish, but it is more convenient to split the cooking process as I have.

Recommended wine – Minervois

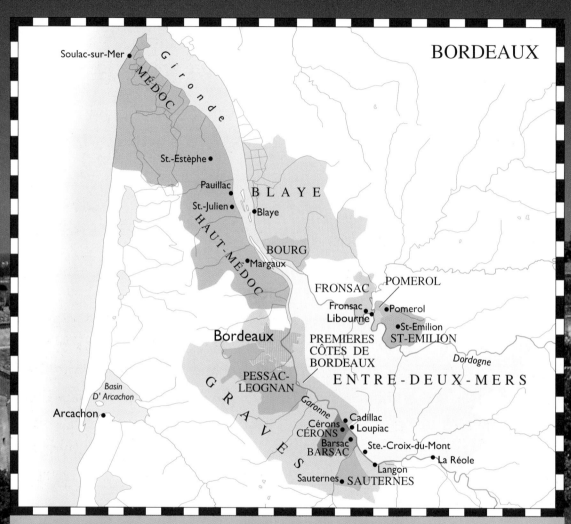

BORDEAUX

Soulac-sur-Mer

Gironde

MÉDOC

St.-Estèphe

BLAYE

Pauillac

St.-Julien
• Blaye

HAUT-MÉDOC

BOURG

Margaux

FRONSAC   POMEROL

Fronsac
Libourne   •Pomerol

Bordeaux   •St-Emilion
            ST-EMILION

PREMIÈRES
CÔTES DE
BORDEAUX   *Dordogne*

PESSAC-
LEOGNAN   ENTRE-DEUX-MERS

*Basin
D'Arcachon*

GRAVES   *Garonne*

Arcachon   Cadillac
            Cérons •Loupiac
            CÉRONS
            Barsac   Ste.-Croix-du-Mont
            BARSAC   •La Réole
                     Langon
            Sauternes SAUTERNES

THE BORDEAUX WINE REGION

BORDEAUX

Fanatical fans of Burgundy (or Australia's Coonawarra, or California's Napa) may raise objections, but I think it is still possible to claim that Bordeaux is the region producing the finest wines in the world. What is more, unlike many wine regions, it actually produces quite large quantities of these fine wines.

From a scenic point of view, most parts of the Bordeaux region are not particularly thrilling. In winter the Médoc can feel very remote and windswept, despite its clutch of fine châteaux. The city of Bordeaux boasts a number of grand public buildings, in particular the Grand Théâtre, and the region does possess a gem in the shape of the medieval town of Saint-Emilion (seen here). Running down a limestone escarpment, the little town has retained much of its charm despite the volume of visitors.

Familiarity with, and the quality reputation of Bordeaux wines in the English-speaking world doubtless has something to do with the close ties that existed in the past between Bordeaux and the British Isles. Central to this was the marriage in 1152 of Eleanor of Aquitaine and Henry Plantagenet. Eleanor controlled much of south west France, including Bordeaux. Henry's lands lay in the Loire, but soon after his marriage to Eleanor he inherited the throne of England. Bordeaux then remained subject to the Kings of England for the next three hundred years. During this time a huge trade in wine built up between the two and the English acquired a taste for the red wines of Bordeaux. In the Middle Ages these wines were quite pale. The French word for pale red was *clairet*, and the English with their fantastic linguistic skills managed to turn this into 'claret', a moniker which has stuck to this very day.

The English lost Bordeaux in 1453. However, despite this reversal, and various brawls down the centuries, the trading links between Bordeaux and the British Isles have stayed strong.

The wines of Bordeaux

As with all classic wine regions, the climate has a significant impact on the style and quality of Bordeaux wines. The area lies a long way south in France, and enjoys a fairly warm climate. The Atlantic Ocean also exerts a huge influence, however, which has its ups and downs. The moderating effect of the sea ensures that spring frost is not too frequent a problem, and good levels of rainfall reduce the risk of drought. However, this rainfall can sometimes come at exactly the wrong times, for instance during the flowering or the harvest. Bordeaux is very much subject to the vagaries of the weather, and thus there are marked variations in the quantity and quality of its vintages.

The basic appellation covering the whole region is simply AC Bordeaux. This encompasses virtually all conceivable styles of wine, but most AC Bordeaux wines are, in practice, either reds or dry whites. The reds tend to be blended primarily from Merlot and Cabernet Sauvignon, and the dry whites from Sémillon and Sauvignon Blanc. Many basic red AC Bordeaux blends are labelled simply as 'Claret'. There is a slightly superior appellation, AC Bordeaux Supérieur, for those wines which achieve a higher minimum alcohol level.

Médoc and Haut-Médoc

The districts that produce finer wines are scattered throughout the region. Just to the north west of the city of Bordeaux is a peninsula called the Médoc, home to the greatest red wines in the world. Often tough and tannic when young, with bottle age these wines become mellow and complex and the best examples fetch heart-stopping prices at auction. Towards the northern end of the peninsula lie the AC Médoc vineyards, which make some very good wines. However, the spectacular section of vineyards lies closer to Bordeaux itself, and is designated AC Haut-Médoc. The special soil here is gravel, providing excellent drainage, retaining the sun's heat, and restricting vigour and yield through its paucity of organic matter. In this part of Bordeaux the dominant grape is the Cabernet Sauvignon, blended in virtually all

BORDEAUX

The Grand Théâtre in Bordeaux

the great Médoc wines with Merlot and Cabernet Franc. Each grape has positive characteristics which are thought to contribute to the overall blend. The Cabernet Sauvignon provides the tough tannic structure, deep colour and blackcurranty aromas. The Merlot is softer and richer on the mid-palate, having less tannin but more alcohol than the Cabernet Sauvignon. A small amount of Cabernet Franc is used to add a herbal, 'tea leafy' component to the blend. Because these varieties bud, flower and ripen at different times, using all three spreads the risk of a major disaster with the weather.

Inside the Haut-Médoc district there are four villages where the majority of the very finest wines are produced. Each of these villages has its own appellation. Running from north to south these are: St. Estèphe, Pauillac, St. Julien and Margaux.

Within these villages are the actual farms which grow the grapes and make the wine. Where most of the rest of France gets by with using the word 'domaines' for its wine-producing farms, in Bordeaux they are almost invariably referred to as 'châteaux'. Several do, in fact, have very grand houses on the estate. Now there is a fair chance that if a wine comes from a château in, say, the village of Pauillac, it will be good. But will it be as good as a wine from the next farm along, also in Pauillac? And will these two wines be as good as those produced by the châteaux on the opposite side of the village? Down the centuries, many consumers have been faced with the same difficulty of trying to get to grips with the relative quality of the top Bordeaux wines. Several brave souls have sat down from time to time in a smoke-filled room, with a blank piece of paper, and tried to draw up a league table of the top châteaux. The most famous of these classifications was made in 1855. Fifty-eight châteaux were judged to be making very fine wines. These châteaux were then slotted into five league divisions. The highest division was that of the Premiers Crus Classés ('First Growths'), followed by the Deuxièmes Crus Classés ('Second Growths'), and so on down to the Fifth Growths. The five properties classified as Premiers Crus Classés are Château Lafite, Château Latour, Château Mouton-Rothschild (elevated to the position in 1973), Château Margaux and Château Haut-Brion. The first three are all AC Pauillac and

Château Margaux is obviously AC Margaux. Château Haut Brion is the oddity in actually coming from part of Graves (see below), and having the AC Pessac-Léognan.

Below the rarefied heights of the Crus Classés are a collection of châteaux rated as Cru Bourgeois. These are often very good wines, and usually sell for considerably less than their aristocratic neighbours.

For those who seek value for money, it is worth noting that most fancy châteaux, as well as making their top wine, also produce a second label. This is often produced from young vines, or from plots which are judged to make wines that are not quite good enough to go into the prestige label. These 'Second Wines' can still be very good, but will sell for much less than the main label.

Those châteaux in the region producing everyday wines at everyday prices are often referred to as 'petits châteaux'.

Graves

On the opposite side of the city of Bordeaux to the Médoc lies the Graves district. The name of the district actually means 'gravel' in French, indicating that it has a similar soil to the Médoc. However, unlike the Médoc appellations which only cover red wine, the AC Graves takes in dry whites as well as reds. The grape mix for the red wines is the same as for the Médoc. The whites are a blend of Sémillon and Sauvignon Blanc. The Sémillon provides the broadness and weight in the

Maturation

After fermentation, wines are racked off their lees and can then be matured. The traditional process involves putting the wine into oak casks to mature. In Bordeaux, the 225 litre small oak barrel used is called a 'barrique'. With oak maturation, the winemaker has to consider a number of important variables. The younger and smaller the cask, the stronger the oak flavour imparted to the wine. The type of oak used is also important – American oak tends to have a more pronounced 'vanilla' aroma than French oak – as is the way the barrels are made: the amount of heat used when the staves are bent affects the wine's flavour. Even the frequency of topping up a barrel to compensate for evaporation can influence a wine's development.

No nails, no glue – just wood, metal hoops and the cooper's skill

Because of their delicacy, white wines which are aged in oak are often only left in barrel for about six months. A classic red Bordeaux, by contrast, might be left for two years in 'barrique'. In this case, because the wine gradually throws a sediment, it may be necessary to rack the casks every three months or so. Nowadays, a lot of wine receives little or no oak ageing. There are two main reasons for this. Firstly, new oak barrels are very expensive, and a distinct oak flavour only tends to come from a cask the first three times it is used. After that, it can serve as a storage vessel, but no obvious oakiness will be transferred to the wine. Secondly, many wines are not improved by oak ageing. For instance, the Riesling grape produces exquisitely fruity white wines and oak ageing would overwhelm this delicate character.

The tombs of Henry Plantaganet and Eleanor of Aquitaine in the Abbey of Fontevraud

FLOYD UNCORKED

Noble Rot

Noble rot is the freakish vine disease which allows the production of many of the world's great sweet wines. The infection of grapes by a mould called *Botrytis cinerea* is usually a disaster (see Hazards in vine growing – Diseases, page 117). However, in certain parts of the world the infection can have an extremely beneficial outcome. If

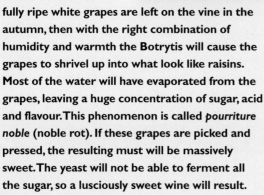

fully ripe white grapes are left on the vine in the autumn, then with the right combination of humidity and warmth the Botrytis will cause the grapes to shrivel up into what look like raisins. Most of the water will have evaporated from the grapes, leaving a huge concentration of sugar, acid and flavour. This phenomenon is called *pourriture noble* (noble rot). If these grapes are picked and pressed, the resulting must will be massively sweet. The yeast will not be able to ferment all the sugar, so a lusciously sweet wine will result.

The rub with noble rot wines is that they are very expensive to make. Firstly, the appearance of noble rot is dependent on the right balance of humidity and warmth. Even in a classic sweet wine area like Sauternes, the ideal weather does not occur with any degree of regularity. Even when it happens, only some grapes on a bunch are affected at any one time. This means that the noble rot-affected berries have to be picked one at a time. What is more, it may be necessary to make up to a dozen sweeps through the vineyards over a period of several weeks to catch all the grapes at the ideal moment. As if all this was not enough, the desiccated berries only release a small amount of juice when pressed! All in all, if there is one wine whose price you should not complain about, it is Sauternes.

blend, the Sauvignon Blanc the crisp fruit and zip of acidity. The best wines in the Graves tend to come from châteaux located close to the southern edge of the city of Bordeaux. A few years ago this sub-district was granted its own appellation, Pessac-Léognan. As mentioned earlier, this area is home to the most famous Graves estate, Château Haut-Brion.

Sauternes and Barsac

Towards the southern end of the Graves are two very famous appellations, Sauternes and Barsac. AC Sauternes and AC Barsac are designations for sweet white wines only. Whilst they use the same

Sémillon/Sauvignon Blanc grape mix as the Graves, in great vintages noble rot will attack the Sémillon grape (see 'Noble Rot', above). It has always been something of a mystery as to why Sauternes and Barsac should be so prone to noble rot, as opposed to anywhere else in the Graves. The climate in this particular corner of Bordeaux seems to favour it, not least because the local rivers generate a lot of autumn mists. The significant clay content in the soil may also help the spread of noble rot by maintaining a high humidity level in the vineyards. Although Sauternes and Barsac will be invariably luscious and intensely sweet, the freshness of the Sauvignon Blanc should always provide balance, and prevent the wines from being cloying. The

SWEET WINES

Many white and rosé wines are made in a medium or sweet style. What you are never allowed to do is just to take a dry wine and add sugar. There are several ways of producing a wine with residual sugar.

1. If grapes contain very high levels of sugar when harvested, then the yeast may not be able to ferment all the sugar into alcohol. This is most famously achieved in areas like Sauternes where the grapes are subject to noble rot. Very high sugar levels can also be generated if the grapes undergo some form of drying after harvest. A small amount of sweet wine is made like this in the Jura region of eastern France.

2. Considerably cheaper than the above is to sweeten a dry wine just before bottling. Unfermented grape juice is widely used for this purpose in Germany (where it is known as *süssreserve*). Grape juice can be reduced to a neutral syrup called 'Rectified Concentrated Must' (RCM). RCM is easy to keep and is used to sweeten table wines.

3. Arresting fermentation before all the sugar has been used up will generate a wine with residual sugar. In the past this was a crude and haphazard process, relying on a fall in the cellar temperature, repeated rackings and the addition of large doses of sulphur dioxide. Refrigeration, centrifugation and filtration can now be deployed to stop fermentation at exactly the right level of residual sugar. This technique has the further advantage of producing a wine with less alcohol than if it had fermented out.

top châteaux in Sauternes and Barsac were classified in 1855, at the same time as the Médoc. However, one estate stood out from all the rest as being in a league of its own. So it was that Château d'Yquem came to be rated Premier Cru Supérieur Classé.

Nearby are some other villages which make sweet white wines. Whilst not usually as rich and complex as Sauternes and Barsac, the wines of AC Cérons, AC Loupiac, AC Sainte-Croix-du-Mont and AC Cadillac can all represent good value for money. One step down from these is AC Premières Côtes de Bordeaux. This strip of vineyards runs along the east side of the River Garonne, and makes everyday medium sweet white wines, as well as a few reds.

Entre-Deux-Mers

Wedged between the Rivers Garonne and Dordogne is a large area of land called the Entre-Deux-Mers ('between the two seas'). Although the AC Entre-Deux-Mers is restricted to dry white wines only, the area also makes a lot of the basic AC Bordeaux reds. Whilst there are few, if any, heroic wines from the Entre-Deux-Mers, many people's main contact with Bordeaux is through honest, simple 'Grocer's Claret', much of which comes from this area.

Saint-Emilion

To the north of the River Dordogne lies the town of Saint-Emilion. AC Saint-Emilion is a designation for red wines only. A fine Saint-Emilion can be as good as a top Médoc, but the wines will be subtly different. There are at least three reasons for this. Firstly, in Saint-Emilion the dominant grape is Merlot, with Cabernet Franc its usual blending partner (unlike the Médoc, where Cabernet Sauvignon is the key player). Secondly, the location of Saint-Emilion, further inland than the Médoc, gives it a summer climate that is fractionally warmer and dryer – the harvest starts slightly earlier here. Thirdly, the soil in most of the best parts of Saint-Emilion is limestone, as opposed to the gravel of the Médoc. When taken together, the result is that a young Saint-Emilion will rarely be as tannic and austere as its cousin from the Médoc, and the telltale blackcurrant aroma of Cabernet Sauvignon is hardly ever encountered, with the herbal character of the Cabernet Franc and the plumminess of the Merlot coming to the fore.

Grape varieties

SÉMILLON The Sémillon grape is the most important white grape grown in Bordeaux. As well as making dry white wines like Graves and Entre-Deux-Mers, it is the key grape used in making Sauternes. Its thin skin predisposes it to attack by noble rot (see 'Noble Rot', page 96), a condition which gives grapes a huge sugar level, permitting the production of a sweet white wine. In Bordeaux it is almost invariably blended with Sauvignon Blanc. The Sémillon is also grown extensively in Australia. In this case it is usually fermented to dryness, with Chardonnay as a regular blending partner.

CABERNET SAUVIGNON If Chardonnay is the most fashionable of the white grapes, then Cabernet Sauvignon is its equivalent amongst the black. On its home patch in Bordeaux, and in particular in the Médoc, it produces wines with a deep colour, intense dark fruit aroma (particularly blackcurrant), and a solid tannic structure. Many people consider these to be the world's greatest red wines, so it should come as no surprise that growers the world over have planted this vine. Particularly strong reputations have been built up by the New World producers, and by the Bulgarians for their inexpensive examples.

MERLOT Although often overshadowed by Cabernet sauvignon, there is actually more Merlot planted in Bordeaux. It tends to dominate the grape mix in Saint-Emilion and Pomerol, and is an important component of most claret blends. The fact that it ripens well before the Cabernet Sauvignon is a distinct advantage in cooler years. Compared to Cabernet Sauvignon, Merlot grapes are less acidic and tannic, and higher in sugar, producing wines that are supple and approachable. Light, quaffable Merlots are produced in Italy, Chile and Eastern Europe. The Californian interpretation is more solid and structured.

One of the vineyards in Saint-Emilion with the town's church beyond

Although generally approachable earlier than a Médoc, a good Saint-Emilion can also keep very well. The top châteaux in Saint-Emilion were not classified until 1955, a century after the Médoc. The two leading estates are Château Ausone and Château Cheval Blanc.

Pomerol

Directly adjoining the vineyards of Saint-Emilion are those of Pomerol. Pomerol has the same sort of climate and grape mix as its neighbour and, as with Saint-Emilion, the AC Pomerol is for red wine only. There is no official classification for the leading châteaux in Pomerol, but this does not seem to have held the area back in any way. In fact, a combination of high quality and tiny production volumes has resulted in record-breaking prices for some of the top wines. Château Pétrus and Le Pin are its two most famous 'cult' wines.

Fronsac, Bourg and Blaye

Not very far from Saint-Emilion and Pomerol is another red wine-only district, called Fronsac. Although not capable of producing wines of the quality of the great Saint-Emilions and Pomerols, there are some decent, moderately priced wines to be found within AC Fronsac.

Northwest of Fronsac, and directly opposite the Médoc, are the two areas of AC Côtes de Bourg and AC Premières Côtes de Blaye. These appellations produce decent, inexpensive reds and dry whites for everyday drinking.

Storing wine at home

Most of the wine that is bought by the average consumer will be drunk within a few days, if not a few hours, of purchase. Mindful of this, the vast majority of retailers stock wines which are ready to drink straight away. Many winemakers have adapted their production techniques to make wines that are approachable young. In the case of a red wine, reducing its tannin content, and emphasising its fruit character, will tend to make it immediately gluggable.

So the good news is that very few wines actually need extended storage at home. In fact, the vast majority of light, fruity wines would be ruined by being kept for too long. However, a number of the classic red wines, and a few top white wines, will benefit from some bottle ageing. A good Médoc or Red Burgundy, or a fine Sauternes, are the sort of wines worth keeping. The reason for this is that a wine's character changes during maturation in the bottle. The smell of a young wine tends to be dominated by fruit and floral aromas; it can, however, be rather closed or 'dumb' on the nose. With age, the wine loses some of its fruitiness, but can open up and start to show more mellow, earthy, leathery, vegetal characteristics. Once it has acquired these sorts of smell a wine is described as having a 'bouquet', as opposed to the youthful fruitiness which is called 'aroma'. In the case of red wines, the tannins change character with bottle age, losing some of their aggressive astringency.

If you do want to keep wine for a few years, the ground rules are very simple. The wine needs to be kept in a place which has an even, cool temperature. Around 12°C is ideal, but slightly warmer is still acceptable. Violent fluctuations of temperature are not (which normally rules out both the garage and the kitchen). Light, high humidity and vibration should be avoided. The bottles should be stored on their sides to make sure that the corks stay moist and maintain a good

seal. The best option in many modern houses, which do not have cellars, is under the stairs.

There is no easy answer to the question of how long a wine should be kept. Some drinkers like the direct fruitiness of a young red wine, in spite of the toughness of the tannins. Other people prefer the mellow earthiness that comes with age. The fun way to tackle this perplexing question is to buy at least three bottles of a favourite red wine. Drink one immediately, but then keep the others, opening one after say two years, and the third after four years. Write a tasting note for each bottle. You will then be able to see how the wine changes during its maturation. Fascinating as this exercise can be in itself, it will also give you a feel for whether you prefer youthful or aged red wines. Of course you could end up keeping a wine for too long. Sad as this is, the chastening experience tends to prevent it happening too frequently!

Decanting

Given that very few wines nowadays need cellaring at home, it should come as little surprise that even fewer will need decanting. It is only the very fullest-bodied, unfiltered red wines that are likely to throw a sediment and therefore need decanting. Subscribers to the 'letting a wine breathe' school might also wish to decant for the added aeration that results.

If a wine is to be decanted, have the bottle standing upright for a couple of days to let any loose sediment sink to the bottom. It is also a good idea to cut off the wine's capsule at the beginning of the two days to avoid shaking the bottle just before the actual decanting. After the two days, remove the cork from the bottle, whilst keeping the bottle as still as possible. Then gently pour the wine from the bottle into the decanter. A clean jug, carafe or empty bottle will be fine if you do not have a decanter. Keep an eye on the wine as it comes out of the bottle, and stop pouring as soon as you see any sediment. With very dark bottles, a candle placed underneath the neck of the bottle when viewed from above will allow you to see the first sign of any sediment coming through. Remember that because wines are usually stored label uppermost, most of the sediment should lie opposite the label. Hence it is best to hold the bottle label uppermost as you decant. The small amount of wine and sediment left at the bottom of the bottle can be ditched or used in cooking. The truly desperate can filter the dregs through a coffee filter, or, indeed, a pair of (clean) old tights.

Château Cantenac-Brown, one of the leading estates in the appellation of Margaux

FLOYD UNCORKED

WINE TASTING NOTES

MEDOC

Floyd "To many, the wines of Bordeaux are the greatest in the world. I am not so sure that, unless you spend a great deal of money, you are going to get good value. However, this particular wine, although too young for my liking, and with a bit too much tannin and oak, to my delight (and I hope the editor of Pseud's Corner reads this) truly tasted of exotic fruit."

Pedley "Deepish mahogany body. Mid-breadth ruby rim. Quite intense but mellow on the nose. Some dark fruit character, in particular blackcurrant. Liquorice, dry leaves, peat and cigar box characteristics as well. A complex bouquet. Dry, mid acidity and moderate alcohol. Quite a grip of dry, cedary tannins. Mid-bodied. Tight, minerally texture in the mouth. A long, chewy finish."

SAUTERNES

Floyd "This is the queen of sweet French wines (though the heady Muscat de Beaumes de Venise from the Rhône is absolutely super, if not as exalted). The moderately priced example I tried tasted of apricots and peaches, notched up 14% alcohol, and felt quite thick and jolly good. You can, of course, spend outrageous sums of money on the finest Sauternes."

Pedley "A full golden colour. Very viscous. The aroma is rich, honeyed and lush. Intense lime marmalade and raisin character. Sweet, with moderate underpinning acidity and high alcohol. Very full-bodied for a white wine. Balanced on the finish."

SAINT-EMILION

Pedley "Mid-deep garnet body. Mid garnet brick rim. Quite intense, open, earthy, meaty nose. Prunes and plums. Fruit cake. Dry, mid acidity, mid-high alcohol. Moderate to soft tannins. Not massive on the palate, rather mid-bodied. Some woody, dried fruit character on the finish."

ENTRE-DEUX-MERS

Pedley "Very pale watery lemon. Crisp at first, but with quite a light intensity. Just a touch of broad green fruit. Pears. Dry, mid-high acidity, moderate alcohol. Fresh and tart. Light-bodied. No great length of flavour."

Floyd food notes

Ahhh! Bordeaux is French for claret – which is therefore uniquely British. In 1152 Eleanor (Rigby – Oh, where do all the lonely people come from...or whatever) from Aquitaine married Henry II, thus giving the English the right to know more about Bordeaux wines and even to own quite a lot. But then, so did the Irish – Château Lynch-Bages is but one, a famous wine owned by Irish wine entrepreneurs, known as the Wild Geese. Hennessy Cognac was born of a ribald relationship between an Irish remittance man of a noble family and a comely, aristocratic French Mademoiselle. I have no doubt that JP, in his elaborate notes, will enlarge on this perception of Bordeaux wines.

Over the several hundred years that the English owned Aquitaine, and were the greatest quaffers of claret (Elizabeth I was known to enjoy the odd drop), they also spent a lot of time building huge castles. I recall one day enjoying a bottle of Pétrus 1962, one of the grandest of all clarets, in the Vieux Logis in Trémolat – which, admittedly, is in the Dordogne, but still heavily influenced by the Bordeaux region. I had just finished a plate of *Pommes Sarladaises*, which is basically a frightfully simple dish of partly sautéd and partly steamed potatoes with truffles, and I was debating whether to have a distinguished little bottle of Cheval Blanc (not actually a whisky, but one of the finest white wines of Bordeaux) with my *Tarte aux Cèpes* or whether to go for a modest Monbazillac – a sweet wine – with a wedge of foie gras in Sauternes jelly. I was ruminating over these important issues with the owner, Bernard, when he said, 'It's strange, isn't it? You English spent hundreds of years here building castles, but you never learnt to cook. If only you had spent as much time learning how to make salads with walnut oil, and sauces with finely chopped shallots and beef marrow and what you call claret, red or white (obviously the nub of Bordelais cooking); if only you had learnt how to make foie gras or goose confit or indeed how to grill a thick piece of rib steak over old vine cuttings *à la Bordelaise...*'
'Ah well,' he sighed, as he quaffed half of my Cheval Blanc, 'at least you have Wimbledon, Daimlers and Rolls Royce'. (Well, we did then!) Anyway, Bordeaux, its wine and its food have been extensively chronicled. There are a million books, a million recipes and a million wines. But then, as Bernard and I sipped some old Cognac followed by some old Armagnac, it

occurred to me that the classic recipe featured here cannot, by law – thanks to the EU – be prepared in Britain. You can only buy marrowbones for your dog, offal like heart is virtually unobtainable, and possibly illegal, and the Brussels gastronomic Star Chamber will probably have you hung, drawn and quartered for trying to enjoy yourself. But don't worry: if you want to eat and drink fine things, just travel to France, Spain or Italy. They don't give a toss about the absurd, grey, pot-bellied food Gestapo of Brussels. The undersized Dover sole so beloved of the Bordelais are known locally as Lawyers' Tongues; any French lawyer who enjoys his food and drink will, like any French housewife, put gastronomic pleasure and satisfaction before European political correctness.

In Saint-Emilion, at the Hostellerie de Plaisance, I had the most brilliant dessert which reminded me of one of the earliest gastronomic experiences I ever had, in the very early '60s, at George Perry-Smith's famous Bath restaurant, The Hole in the Wall. His speciality, as a true disciple of Elizabeth David's 'French Provincial Cooking', was Chocolate St-Emilion, a rich, dark chocolate mousse poured over crunchy macaroons soaked in Armagnac. At the Hostellerie they created a similar, but more refined delight of macaroons with a praline cream (*Macaron à la crème praline*) and it was truly exquisite.

Heading off east on the D936 I came across one of those accidents of life that can alter your mind. In a simple courtyard, on a soft-scented August night, at a modest roadside hotel called Hotel aux Deux Grands Nichons, they were serving chocolate mousse with macaroons à la Elizabeth David. The *Entrecote à la Bordelaise* was cooked unfussily over a *feu de bois* of old vine cuttings. It was coated in a rich shallot and St-Emilion wine sauce thick with marrow and served with one of the most amazing little wines I have ever tried in my life, called Haute Colombe Hector, 1974. And for once on my journeys the whole thing did not cost an arm and a leg.

Entrecote bordelaise

(Char-grilled rib cut steak with beef marrow and a red wine sauce)

FOR THE DEMI-GLACE:

1 onion, peeled

1 leek, trimmed

1 carrot

2 or 3 sprigs of fresh thyme

1 bayleaf

2 pig's trotters

1 ox heart

red wine or water to cover

1 tablespoon butter

1 tablespoon flour

FOR THE STEAKS AND SAUCE:

8 well-hung entrecote (rib cut) steaks, or any cut of steak suitable for grilling

6 shallots, very finely chopped

50 g/1¾ oz butter

half a bottle of claret

a couple of sprigs of fresh thyme

2–3 bayleaves

250ml/9 fl oz demi-glace (see method)

a large knob of butter

100 g/3½ oz marrow from a beef bone

oil for grilling

salt and pepper

Serves 8

You will need a natural charcoal barbecue (the French like to use dried vine cuttings). If you're in a hurry, you can buy a ready-made red wine sauce in the supermarket instead of making your own demi-glace, but I'm going to give you a simple and effective way of making this multi-purpose sauce.

If you are making your own demi-glace, do this first. Place all the ingredients apart from the butter and flour in a casserole, bring to the boil and simmer for 2 or 3 hours. Strain off the liquid and freeze half of it for another dish. Feed the heart to your pet dog and discard the rest of the solids. In a separate saucepan, melt the butter and stir in the flour, mixing well over a low heat until the paste is cooked but not brown. Gradually add the hot liquid, stirring all the time, until you have a smooth sauce.

Fire up your barbecue and make sure your steaks are at room temperature for cooking. Sauté the shallots until golden in the butter, add the wine and herbs and boil furiously until the liquid is reduced by half, then add the demi-glace and bring to the boil again. Remove the herbs and whisk in a knob of butter to make a smooth, rich, wine-flavoured sauce.

FOR THE GARNISH:

**a couple of bunches of
watercress, washed and trimmed**

**pommes allumettes (deep-fried
matchstick potatoes)**

Recommended wine - Claret

Just before cooking the steaks, poach the marrow in the sauce for 2–3 minutes until tender. Remove the marrow from the sauce, cut it into eight slices, season with salt and pepper and set aside until ready to serve. Brush the steaks with oil. Whack the steaks on the barbecue and grill to your liking. When they are cooked, heat the marrow through in the sauce and place one piece on top of each steak. Spoon the sauce over the steaks and serve at once with watercress and *pommes allumettes*.

ALSACE

The Alsace AOC zone

Strasbourg

VOSGES MOUNTAINS

Bergheim

Riquewihr

Colmar

Rhine

Freiburg

FRANCE
GERMANY

Mulhouse

THE ALSACE WINE
REGION

VINS D'ALSACE
A 100 H.

VINS D'ALSACE

ALSACE

*A*lsace is always one of the most magical parts of France to visit. On a clear day, from the vineyards one can see over the River Rhine and into Germany. In Alsace you feel close to the heart of Europe. Given its position on the border of France and Germany, it is no surprise that the area has a fascinating, hybrid culture. Much of the architecture has a medieval German feel to it, and the villages, like Riquewihr (seen here) and Bergheim, virtually all have German-sounding names. There is, however, a tragic side to Alsace's geographical position. Many wars have been fought across its fields and vineyards, and sovereignty has changed four times in the twentieth century alone.

Geography, and in particular its influence on climate, is also at the heart of what makes the wines of Alsace distinctive. The northern position of Alsace dictates that it should primarily be a white wine producing region, as most black grapes would never ripen in such cool conditions. To afford some protection from spring frost the vines are trained slightly higher above the ground than elsewhere in northern France. As well as being cool, Alsace is also very dry, due to its separation from the rest of France by a sizeable mountain range, the Vosges. These mountains, lying to the west of Alsace, cut out a lot of the rain clouds which come in from the Atlantic. The autumns, in particular, are often fine and dry, allowing the white grapes to ripen fully, whilst retaining a crisp backbone of acidity. In fact it is hard to conceive of a better climate for growing high quality white wines.

The wines of Alsace

The primeval forces which formed the Vosges millions of years ago also caused numerous geological faults across the Alsace region, creating a huge range of soil types, often within the same village. Most Alsace wines are blended from the grapes of several vineyards, so soil-generated distinctions will not be apparent. On the other hand, these variations of soil type, within a few hundred metres of each other, allow those growers who take pride in the concept of *terroir* to make individual wines which reflect the characteristics of each site.

The white wines of Alsace differ in one crucial respect from those produced over the border in Germany: the vast majority are dry, whereas a lot of exported German wine tends to be medium sweet. Confusingly, Alsatian winemakers are compelled by law to bottle their wine in green *flûtes d'Alsace* which look very Germanic. This leaves the consumer confronted with a bottle whose appearance misleadingly suggests its contents are medium sweet, creating something of a marketing problem.

Appellations

One aspect of Alsace wine which is not confusing at all is the appellation system for the region. Almost all Alsace wine sells simply as AC Alsace. It is only comparatively recently that the system was modified to allow the best vineyards a higher rating. Now, if a wine comes from one of the top fifty vineyards in the region, it can be sold as AC Alsace Grand Cru. As you might expect from such a cool region, most of these special sites are found on the south or south-east facing slopes of the Vosges. The only other appellation that one sees occasionally is AC Crémant d'Alsace, which covers the small amount of sparkling wine made in the region.

You are probably thinking that there must be a catch somewhere. On the face of it, no. Virtually all

ALSACE

Alsace wine labels tell you the name of the grape from which the wine has been made. Indeed, Alsace was one of the world's first winemaking regions to adopt this simple, varietal approach to labelling, now so familiar to most consumers. The only slight problem is that there are as many as eight different grape varieties in Alsace, most of which are regularly used to produce varietal wines.

ASPECT

The aspect of a vineyard can be crucial. The degree of exposure to sun, rain, wind and frost can make huge differences in the size and quality of a harvest. In northern Europe, the best vineyards are often located on slopes, optimising exposure to the sun, drainage and shelter, and minimising the risk of frost. The climate experienced by an individual vineyard is referred to as its microclimate (or more correctly its mesoclimate).

Gewürztraminer

The grape which automatically comes to mind in the context of Alsace is the Gewürztraminer. Although grown elsewhere in the world, it is Alsace which unquestionably produces the benchmark examples. Of all the white grapes, it is the Gewürztraminer which produces the most perfumed and scented wines ('Gewürz' is the German word for spice). Its intense floral character, allied with richness on the palate, tends to be something you either love or hate. Those same qualities have led Gewürztraminer to being a recommended partner for a number of Chinese and Indian dishes, as well as smoked fish and

meat. Keith is not convinced that it goes that well with Asian cuisine, but it may be something worth trying out for yourself at home or in a restaurant.

Riesling

Popular as Gewürztraminer is, a lot of people would claim that Riesling actually produces the greatest wine in Alsace. When young, Alsace Riesling can be rather austere, with initially delicate green fruit barely disguising the often searing acidity. However, with a few years of bottle age, the nose broadens out, the classic 'petrol' bouquet develops, and the wine seems more mellow. Because of this fruit intensity and high acidity, a top Alsace Riesling can keep for many years, in marked contrast to the Gewürztraminer, whose perfumed character can fade in the bottle. The classic food pairing for Alsatian Riesling is trout.

Pinot Gris

Alsace is also capable of producing some excellent wines from the Pinot Gris grape. The Pinot Gris gives wines which can be rich and oily on the palate, and like Gewürztraminer, quite high in alcohol. Where they differ is in the absence of any exotic aroma. Rather, one tends to get a broad, ripe, heaviness on the nose, which is hard to describe in terms of specific fruit characteristics. Until recently, Alsace Pinot Gris was often called 'Tokay d'Alsace', a reference to Hungary's great sweet wine. There are various theories as to the origin of the name but it is certainly the case that no Pinot Gris finds its way into present-day Hungarian Tokaji. Recent regulations stipulate that the name 'Tokay d'Alsace' is no longer permitted, but a number of people still refer to the wine as 'Tokay-Pinot Gris'. Given the paucity of red wine in Alsace, Pinot Gris, with its richness on both the nose and the palate, is often recommended there as an accompaniment to meat dishes, even game.

Other grapes

The Muscat grape is usually associated with the production of sweet wines. However, in Alsace it is used to make a delicate, dry, floral white wine. Pinot Blanc is the grape currently favoured for everyday wine production. Most versions have a simple, light fruitiness on the nose, and a light, clean palate. It is a shame that more wine bars do not serve it by the glass. The Sylvaner, which generally produces a rather neutral dry white wine, seems to have few friends at the moment. The Chasselas grape is primarily a table grape, and is fast disappearing from the Alsace vineyards. The odd man out in this white wine region is the Pinot Noir, which is used to produce a light and fruity red wine, with a much more marked acidity than red Burgundy.

Late harvest wines

If you get into Alsace wine in a big way, there are a couple of special wines that are worth looking out for. They can be expensive, but can equally well prove fantastic. If there is a fine autumn in Alsace, with good weather up until the end of October, some growers will delay picking their grapes by a couple of weeks. This will allow the grapes to ripen further, and to have quite a high sugar content when picked. The resulting wine, designated 'Vendange Tardive' (late harvest) will be richer and more intense than a normal Alsace wine. Some are fermented dry, whereas others may have a little sugar left over and are medium. In really fantastic years, some of these late-harvested grapes may be infected with noble rot (see 'Noble rot', page 96). These lusciously sweet grapes allow the production of a tiny amount of sweet wine, sold as 'Sélection de Grains Nobles'.

Given the sheer quality and reliability of Alsace wines, and their generally moderate prices, there can only be one piece of advice: drink more of them.

Grape varieties: Riesling

The Riesling is arguably the most aristocratic of all the world's white grape varieties. Yet for many consumers the word 'Riesling' conjures up memories of grim, inexpensive plonk, thanks largely to confusion with a lesser grape called Laski Riesling and to the poor image of mass-market German wine. As well as being Germany's most prestigious grape, Riesling also produces some very fine wines in Alsace. Whilst many of the German Rieslings are medium or even sweet, in Alsace the winemakers go for a drier style. When young, Riesling has a crisp, appley aroma. With age, an extraordinary complex bouquet develops, often exhibiting what is considered to be a classic 'petrolly' character.

BOTTLING

Anyone who finds bottling lines exciting probably has a major personality defect. Some go very fast and some go slowly, but the end result is the same – they all get the wine into the bottle. That said, a lot of skill and technology go into making sure that contamination from the atmosphere, or from dirty bottles, or from the wine itself, is kept to a minimum. In addition, contact with the air has to be minimised to prevent the wine from deteriorating.

Most bottles of wine are still closed with cork, which is made from the bark of a special type of oak tree. Whilst a good quality cork is an excellent way of sealing a bottle, natural cork is not without its problems. It has become very expensive over the last few years, yet despite the price increases, the quality of many corks is suspect. A poor cork will allow air into the bottle, ultimately destroying the wine. Even more worrying is the incidence of 'cork taint'. Some corks, perhaps through mould infections or treatments during manufacture, can impart a disgusting, mouldy, dusty smell to the wine. This is what is meant by the term 'corked' wine (not that little fragments of cork are floating around in the glass).

For these reasons, wine producers have investigated various other types of closure. Screw top bottles are fine for everyday wines, but unfortunately have a naff image. There is a lot of interest at the moment in synthetic corks, which can be made to look like the real thing, whilst behaving more consistently.

Bottles of course are not the only way of packaging wine; other formats include bag-in-box and cans.

The thrilling sight of a bottling line

Hazards in vine growing

Between pruning the vines in February, and harvesting the grapes in September, much of the grape grower's year is spent trying to fend off various threats to his vines. The principal problems facing a vine grower, and the measures taken to combat them, are as follows:

WEATHER PROBLEMS

Winter Frost

At temperatures below minus 20°C the vine will freeze and die. Although this problem is rare in most vineyard regions, when it does occur whole vineyards can be destroyed. Given the cost of replanting a vineyard from scratch, it can take several years for a region or individual grower to recover. Ploughing earth over the trunks of the vines in the autumn affords some protection.

Grey rot destroying a bunch of Pinot Noir grapes

Spring Frost

Vines are particularly susceptible to frost damage once the buds have burst in the spring. Temperatures just below 0°C can kill the tender shoots, destroying the embryonic flowers. Fewer surviving flowers means fewer bunches of grapes. Most of a year's crop can be lost in this way, although the vines usually recover in time for the next growing season. Heaters or fans in the vineyard can prevent the freezing air from settling on the vines. Spraying the vines with water (aspersion) is also highly effective.

Coulure and *Millerandage*

Unsettled weather at flowering time can cause 'floral abortion' and 'failure of grape set' ('coulure' and 'millerandage' are the French technical terms for these problems). The result is an unintentionally reduced crop. Some grape varieties, such as Merlot, are more prone to these problems than others.

Drought

During a period of prolonged drought the grapes stop ripening. Young vines with limited root penetration can die.

Hail

Hail can damage leaf and shoot growth, and bruise the fruit. The latter is then susceptible to rot infection. The one way to try to stave off this problem is to fire rockets into the clouds. The rockets cause the moisture in the cloud to fall as rain rather than as destructive hail.

Rain at Harvest

Even if the year has gone well up to the end of August, the quality of the vintage can still be spoilt by heavy rain in September. The vines take up the water, swelling the grapes and diluting their sugar, acidity and flavour. If it is warm as well as humid, then grey rot can attack the grapes and destroy them.

DISEASES

Grey Rot

Grey rot (also known as bunch rot) can be a major problem as the grapes approach ripeness. The fungus *Botrytis cinerea* attacks the skin of the grape (see left), destroying its structure and pigmentation. Destructive enzymes are produced, and the skin damage allows secondary infections. It is virtually impossible to make satisfactory wines from rotten grapes. Control is difficult, with *Botrytis* rapidly becoming resistant to fungicidal sprays. Whilst grey rot is extremely destructive, the same mould, under different circumstances, is responsible for noble rot (see 'Noble rot', page 96).

Mildew

Two types of mildew can cause the grape-grower problems: downy mildew and powdery mildew. Both attack all the green parts of the vine, destroying shoots, leaves, flowers and fruit. Synthetic treatment sprays are available, but two traditional preventative sprays are still widely used: Bordeaux mixture (copper sulphate, lime and water) to control downy mildew, and sulphur to prevent powdery mildew.

WINE TASTING NOTES

RIESLING

Floyd "At its best, a very crisp and fruity wine that is sometimes thick to swallow and has, for me, the taste of lemon cream — I like it very much. I think it goes particularly well with pasta, onion tarts, quiches, and vegetable dishes like potato gratin or cauliflower cheese."

Pedley "Palish straw appearance. Fairly intense aroma. Sharp, fresh and clean. Lemons and green apples. Even some pineapple. Dryish, with high acidity and moderate alcohol. Light-bodied and crisp. Elegant rather than massive. A fine flavour. N.B. With bottle age, Alsace Riesling develops an incredible 'petrolly' bouquet."

GEWURZTRAMINER

Floyd "At the expensive end, this can be quite a sweet wine. I tried one that tasted slightly of lychees and was good and throaty...an excellent all-day drinking wine and good with things like foie gras, sweet brioches, and really soft, pongy cheeses. Not for fish, but roast chicken, yes. It is a wine that is as good as the money you spend on it."

Pedley "Bright, mid-gold colour. Big, rich, powerful aroma. A huge concentration of fruit, in particular lychees. Also quite scented and floral, with hints of rose and hyacinth. Off-dry, with only moderate acidity but a high level of alcohol. Very full-bodied and round for a white wine. Almost oily. Fairly long finish."

TOKAY-PINOT GRIS

Pedley "Bright, medium depth of yellow gold on the appearance. Deep and rich on the nose. Very broad and weighty, but as usual with this variety, hard to pick out individual fruit flavours. Perhaps a touch of tropical fruit. Almost medium dry. Mid acidity and very high alcohol. A big wine on the palate. Juicy and deep."

PINOT BLANC

Pedley "Pale watery lemon colour. Light, fresh and clean. Not a particularly intense smell. A youthful wine, showing some fruit, perhaps a hint of banana character. Dry, moderate acidity and moderate alcohol. Fairly light, with a crisp edge. Not particularly long or deep."

FLOYD UNCORKED

Floyd food notes

If there is one region of France that truly merits its gastronomic reputation, it is Alsace. A beautiful region delineated by the brooding Vosges mountains and the majestic River Rhine, Alsace has been French, German, French, German, French, etc, through wars and invasions over the centuries. As a result, Alsatian cooking superficially appears very Germanic. There is a lot of pork and bacon, heavy stews and hotpots, sausages and smoked ham hocks, and wonderful game birds, wild boar and hare. But – and it is a big but – the Germanic influence on this area where cabbage is the queen of vegetables and onion is king, and where rhubarb is honoured alongside blueberries and sweet, succulent wild strawberries, has been lifted to heavenly heights by refined, passionate, articulate cooks. With the force of tradition behind them, they have created *Choucroute* and *Baeckeoffe* – a sort of Lancashire hotpot with pork, mutton, beef and pig's trotters. Inspired by the local wines and the wonderful marcs and eaux-de-vie (spirits) of Alsace, they have come up with familial but exquisite dishes such as *Coq au Riesling*, or fillets of zander (pike-perch) with frogs' legs in a creamy Riesling sauce, or the delicate *matelote*, a delightful fish stew of pike, perch, trout, eel and tench, again lovingly prepared in Riesling. There are exquisite terrines of *foie gras* and wonderful soups based on the famous Alsace beers. There are the much abused, but in Alsace-Lorraine creamy and succulent, quiches and *tartes à l'oignon*, and the finest of onion, bacon and cheese tarts, known as *tarte flambée*, baked in a wood-fired oven. With its thin bread-dough base smeared with cream cheese, crème fraîche, lardons of bacon and onions, molten on top and crisp underneath, this leaves your so-called pizza on the culinary starting block.

In Alsace it is said that any *pâtissier* (pastry chef) can become a cook, but not any cook can become a *pâtissier*. The cakes and tarts and puddings are divine, as are the wonderful brioches, biscuits and breads. It is also said – and I believe it to be true – that good cooks have been trained either as *charcutiers* (the *charcuterie* of Alsace is outstanding) or as *boulangers* (bakers) or *pâtissiers*. As well as the very fine sweet tarts, the wonderfully savoury *tourtes* – really brilliant pasties – are well worth trying.

Alsace seems to have so many fine restaurants, more than any other region of France. Should you find yourself in Ammerschwihr, go to 'Aux Armes de France' and try the *Grenouilles et escargots à la crème de lentilles* (snails and frogs' legs cooked with lentils); or if you are in Villé, at the restaurant 'Au Valet de Coeur' try their *Sandre aux grenouilles fraîches* (zander cooked with frogs' legs, garlic and parsley).

Choucroute Alsacienne
(Pickled cabbage with pork and sausages)

FOR THE CHOUCROUTE:

2.25 kg/5 lb mild choucroute (pickled cabbage, available from large supermarkets – may be labelled 'sauerkraut')

I large onion, finely chopped

225 g/8 oz goose fat or lard

10 or 12 juniper berries

I garlic clove, crushed

I large onion, peeled and stuck with a few cloves

a couple of bottles of Alsace Riesling

salt and pepper

FOR THE MEATS:

2 smoked ham hocks

675 g/1½ lb piece of smoked belly of pork

450 g/1 lb piece of salt belly of pork

900 g/2 lb piece of smoked pork loin

12 Strasbourg sausages

12 white (boudin blanc type) or frankfurter-style sausages

I pig's caul (fatty tissue that surrounds the pig's stomach)

FOR THE VEGETABLES:

2.25 kg/5 lb potatoes, peeled and cut into even-sized pieces

900 g/2 lb carrots, peeled and kept whole

A party pot that serves between eight and fourteen people; needless to say the measurements are approximate as this is a big, fun, winter party dish. The variety of meats needed means there would be absolutely no point in making it for fewer than four people. You will almost certainly need to order the caul in advance from your butcher. If you can't find Strasbourg sausages, use any good quality, pure pork poaching (quick cooking) sausage.

Serves 8 – 14

First, rinse the choucroute in cold water and drain well. Fry the chopped onion in the goose fat or lard in a large casserole until golden. Now add the choucroute, then the juniper berries, the garlic and the onion stuck with cloves. Next add all of the meat with the exception of the sausages. Season lightly with salt, generously with pepper. Cover the lot with the Riesling and if necessary a dash of water, then spread the caul over the top of the ingredients like a hair-net (you may need to soak it in warm water for a few minutes to make it pliable).

Bring the dish to the boil on top of the stove. The second it is boiling, put on the lid and place the casserole in a low oven (170°C/325°F/Gas Mark 3) for about 2 hours. Every now and again you must check that the choucroute is still moist. If necessary add a little more Riesling or water.

After about 1½ hours, boil your potatoes and carrots in the usual way until tender. Strain and keep warm on one side. Next, check that the meats in the choucroute are almost cooked and add the sausages for the last ten minutes or so.

When the dish is ready, remove the meat and sausages, carve the meat into manageable slices and keep both meat and sausages warm while you place the cabbage onto one or more large serving dishes. Then place the meat and sausages on top of the choucroute and arrange the potatoes and the carrots around the edge.

Recommended wine – Riesling

Aisne

•Reims

MONTAGNE
DE
REIMS

VALLÉE DE LA MARNE
•Château-
Thierry   Épernay•

Marne

CÔTE
DES
BLANCS

Châlons-en-Champagne•

Sézanne•

CÔTE DE
SÉZANNE

Romilly-
sur-Seine•

Seine

Brienne-
le-Château•

•Troyes

•Bar-sur-Aube

AUBE VINEYARDS

CHAMPAGNE

——— delimited AOC region
of Champagne

THE CHAMPAGNE WINE REGION

CHAMPAGNE

First-time visitors to the Champagne region are often shocked by just how bleak the landscape is. Compared to many vineyard regions, the countryside responsible for 'The King of Wines' is not the stuff of picture postcards. In many parts of Champagne the nearest thing to a national monument is a grain silo. In Reims Cathedral, shown overleaf, at least the capital of Champagne has what is arguably the most beautiful of all the great French gothic cathedrals, and the Romanesque basilica of Saint-Remi is also very fine.

A further shocking revelation is that Champagne, as you and I know it, is a fairly new-fangled business. Champagne in the seventeenth century was a still wine, and usually red at that (indeed, small quantities of both non-sparkling white and red Champagne are still produced in the region). It seems that like many great discoveries, sparkling Champagne was a bit of a mistake. What may have originally happened is that barrels of still wine were shipped from Champagne before the fermentation was completely finished. If this shipment was in the winter time, the yeast would have been dormant. However, a couple of months later, when the wine had reached its destination and the weather was warmer, the yeast would start to work again. The carbon dioxide produced by this second burst of fermentation would turn the wine fizzy. Rather than being horrified by this bizarre sparkling wine, the aristocracy rapidly adopted Champagne as a fashionable novelty.

The crafting of Champagne

This spontaneous refermentation was clearly somewhat hit and miss. The last three hundred years have seen the process of making the wine fizzy brought under control, and made much more reliable. The man responsible in the early days for a lot of this progress was a monk at the Abbey at Hautvillers. Dom Pérignon was the first Champagne producer to realise that blending wines from different villages gave a more complex wine than that produced from just one. He also established how to instigate a reliable second fermentation in the bottle. (At the time, it was, interestingly, only English-manufactured glass that could stand the pressure of the carbon dioxide.) Since then, various other innovations have streamlined production and made it less labour intensive. However, the basic process of making the wine sparkle by stimulating a second fermentation in the bottle is still used by all Champagnes.

Appellation Contrôlée

Champagne is protected by *Appellation Contrôlée* law in the same way as are France's other classic wine regions. In other words, the wine called Champagne can only come from specified vineyards within the Champagne region. This is important, as in many parts of the world the word 'champagne' has been used to describe locally-produced sparkling wines. The Champenois are very influential, and litigious, so bit by bit we are getting to a position where the name 'Champagne' is protected in virtually all the main markets of the world. Given the importance of *Appellation Contrôlée* in protecting Champagne, it is odd that it is the only AC which does not have to put the words 'Appellation Contrôlée' on the label.

In fact, in the European Union, the protection of the name 'Champagne' has been extended to cover protection of the name of the production process as well, the 'méthode champenoise'. In the past, Cava (the sparkling wine from Spain) and other quality sparkling wines using the same production technique as Champagne, were allowed to style themselves 'méthode champenoise'. This is now illegal, and these other sparkling wines are restricted to using the term 'méthode traditionelle'.

CHAMPAGNE

The gothic splendour of Reims Cathedral

Geography of the region

The Champagne region is the northernmost vineyard area in France, lying 140 kilometres east of Paris, and has an extremely cool climate. (If you think your job is grim, just imagine having to spend day after day in the freezing cold of February doing the pruning.) This cold climate results in wines that are very high in acidity, part of the reason why Champagne can keep well, and one of the elements that distinguishes Champagne from any other sparkling wine. The weather is very variable, resulting in inconsistent crop size and quality from one year to the next. The low lying areas of the region are particularly prone to spring frost damage.

Soil and grapes

Virtually all the vineyards in the Champagne region have chalk as their subsoil. The actual soil layer is very shallow, with light digging often revealing the underlying chalk (as seen below). Until recently, this soil was 'fertilised' by spreading domestic refuse amongst the vines. The shredded bin bag garbage rotted down to provide organic matter for the vines. The unpleasant side of this practice was that the non-biodegradable part of the refuse, primarily plastic and glass, was left littering the vineyards.

Three grape varieties are grown to make

Champagne: Pinot Noir, Pinot Meunier and Chardonnay. Pinot Noir and Pinot Meunier are both black grapes, whereas the Chardonnay is, of course, white. Roughly equal proportions of the three grapes are grown in the region (Pinot Noir has a slightly larger area under vine than the other two). Part of the skill in making Champagne is getting the juice out of the black grapes without picking up any colour.

There are three top quality vineyard districts. The Montagne de Reims is planted mainly with Pinot Noir. The Vallée de la Marne has some Pinot Noir, but is primarily planted with Pinot Meunier. The Côte des Blancs is home to the Chardonnay.

There are some more vineyards to the south in the Aube *département*, but these are generally reckoned to produce lesser wines. Although there are three different grape varieties, grown in three distinct districts, most Champagnes are made by blending together wines from the different grapes and districts. The Pinot Noir is reckoned to provide backbone and structure to the blend. The Chardonnay gives finesse and elegance. The Pinot Meunier has a two-fold function. Firstly, it provides an immediate fruitiness. Secondly, whilst not capable of the quality of the Pinot Noir, its late-budding nature makes it invaluable in vineyards susceptible to spring frost.

THE GRAPE GROWERS

Most of the land in the region is actually owned by individual farmers, rather than by the big Champagne companies. This creates a very important split in responsibility in the industry. The growing of the grapes and the harvesting are primarily in the hands of smallholders. Most of them sell their grapes to the Champagne companies, who make the wine and market it around the world.

There have been some torrid moments in the history of Champagne when these two sides of the industry have fallen out. Understandably enough, the growers want to receive the highest possible price for their grapes, whilst the Champagne companies want to keep the cost of the grapes down. In the past there was a formal system where representatives of the growers and of the Champagne houses agreed a fixed price for the grapes before each harvest. This system has now been abandoned, and it is up to each grower to get the best possible price for his grapes. Not all growers sell their grapes to the big Champagne producers: a sizeable number make and market their own Champagnes while others are members of cooperative wineries.

One important element in determining the price a grower receives for his grapes, or his Champagne, is the reputation of the village where his grapes grow. The Champagne region has an odd system whereby each village is given a percentage score. This system, called the *échelle des crus* (the scale of 'crus'), allocates the top villages a score of 100%. This is equivalent to Grand Cru in other regions of France, and this term is occasionally seen on the label of some Champagnes. Verzenay, Bouzy, Cramant and Avize are four of the most famous Grand Cru villages. Villages allocated a score between 99% and 90% are obviously reckoned to produce grapes that are good, but not quite up to the standard of the 100% villages. They are equivalent to Premier Cru elsewhere, and the term can be shown on the labels of their wines. The lowest score possible is 80%, and villages with a rating between 80% and 89% can be thought of as producing regular quality grapes. The finest, and therefore often the most expensive, Champagnes usually contain a significant proportion of grapes from the Grand Cru villages.

A traditional Champagne press in action

The first fermentation

In the Champagne region all the grapes are picked by hand and are then moved quickly from the vineyard to the press house. The big Champagne companies have press houses scattered throughout the vineyard districts, so the grapes only have to be transported a few kilometres at most. The whole bunches of grapes are then pressed gently to release the juice. This is particularly critical in the case of the black grapes, as it is important that no red colour gets into the juice. The first pressing, called the 'cuvée', gives the finest quality of must. The second pressing releases what is called the 'taille'. These two fractions of must will be fermented separately, and only later will the winemaker decide what should be blended with what.

The must is allowed to settle for a few hours, a process called 'débourbage'. The clear juice is then fermented, just like any other white wine. This fermentation is mainly carried out in stainless steel, although a few producers do still ferment in oak casks. Once fermented, the white wine will be racked and then moved to storage vats. This is the base wine for Champagne, and at this stage it is a viciously acid, still, dry white wine. The winemaker and his team have to start to taste all the different vats of base wine, to form an impression of the characteristics of each one and establish a likely blend.

Non-vintage Champagne

The bread and butter of the Champagne industry is the non-vintage wine. This is produced by selecting a number of vats of the current year's wine, and then adding in some older reserve wines from previous years' harvests to add maturity and complexity to the blend. Dozens of different wines may be combined in the non-vintage blend, usually taking in the three different grapes, the three main districts, and often wines from both *cuvée* and *taille* pressings. Given that continuity is the aim of a non-vintage blend, the reserve wines are also used to help smooth out the huge changes of style and quality that can result from vintage variation.

Vintage Champagne

In very good years, a number of vats of wine may stand out as being particularly fine. The winemaker will set these aside, blend them, but not add any reserve wines. This blend will make the vintage Champagne. Unlike non-vintage Champagne, where uniformity is the aim, the whole point of vintage Champagne is that it should show off the characteristics of the year in question. Nowadays, most Champagne companies also make what is known as a 'Prestige Cuvée' vintage Champagne. This will be a particularly rigorous selection of wines from one year.

Other Champagne styles

Several variations are possible at the blending stage. A Rosé Champagne can be produced by adding red wine to the blend. Traditionally the red wine that is used for the blending comes from the village of Bouzy. This is a bit of a cheat, as most still rosés are made by leaving crushed black grapes in contact with their skins for a few days (see 'Rosé winemaking', page 67). In fact, some Rosé Champagnes are made 'properly' this way. If a blend is made just by using vats of Chardonnay wine, a white-grape-only Champagne will be produced. This will be lighter and more delicate than the traditional three-grape blend, and is often sold as 'Blanc de Blancs'. A few companies make a white Champagne from an all black grape blend, which is sold as 'Blanc de Noirs'.

The second fermentation

Up to this point all the wines are still. The next stage involves getting the sparkle into the wines. However, a small amount of red and of white wine is sold in this non-sparkling state. The AC Coteaux Champenois is

the designation given to these still wines, the most famous being the Pinot Noir-based Bouzy Rouge.

To obtain the sparkle, the blended base wine is mixed with *liqueur de tirage*, which consists of wine, sugar and yeast. The wine is then bottled and taken down into the cellars (the Champagne-producing towns are honeycombed with magnificent caves carved out of the chalk, as can be seen below) where the bottles are stacked on their sides. The essence of the Champagne method is that this wine will not now leave the bottle until you or I pop the cork. The bottles are usually closed at this stage with crown caps which look for all the world like beer bottle tops. With a mixture of sugar and yeast in each bottle, a second fermentation starts. Because of the cool temperature in the cellars this second fermentation takes several weeks. The carbon dioxide produced cannot escape from the bottle, so the wine goes fizzy. The pressure in the bottle rises to six atmospheres (hence the need for a heavy bottle).

Once all the sugar has been used up, the yeast die

and sink to the side of the bottle where they form a sticky deposit. The Champagne is then left maturing in contact with the dead yeast. This maturation gives Champagne its special yeasty flavour, and generally the better the Champagne, the longer it will be left on the yeast lees. The appellation law states that all non-vintage Champagnes should mature for at least fifteen months, and all vintage Champagnes for at least three years. However, most top non-vintage Champagnes will be matured for more like three years, and a good vintage Champagne for five years or more.

Remuage and Dégorgement

Once the maturation is completed, the yeast deposit has to be expelled from the bottle. The first part of this process involves getting the deposit down to the neck of the bottle. It was the widow Clicquot who supposedly figured out how to do this. She had holes drilled in her kitchen table, which she then stood on its end. By placing the bottles in horizontally, old Mrs Clicquot could turn and tip them up a little each day, over a period of several weeks gradually driving the yeast deposit into the necks of the bottles. This process, called remuage, is still partly done by hand even nowadays. Most books will tell you that a good remueur can turn 30,000 bottles a day, but Keith and I met a chap who reckoned he could do 50,000 a day with a following wind! I am not sure what his job satisfaction was though. In fact, much of the remuage has been automated today, with computer controlled 'gyropalettes' turning the bottles several times a day and moving the yeast down to the neck of the bottle in a few days.

With the yeast deposit now located just above the closure, the neck of the bottle is plunged into a bath of freezing salt water. Brine stays liquid at well below 0°C, so it is able to freeze the wine and yeast in the neck of the bottle. With the yeast trapped in this manner, the bottle can now be turned upright. If the crown cap is removed, the six atmospheres of pressure in the bottle fires out the plug of yeast and frozen wine. This process of expelling the yeast is called dégorgement. The bottles

are now open, and some wine has been lost during the disgorging. The bottles are topped up with a mixture called liqueur d'expédition. This consists of reserve wine, into which a small amount of cane sugar has been dissolved – yet another example of how Champagne is allowed to bend the rules (it is normally illegal to sweeten a wine by adding sugar). The more sugar in the liqueur d'expédition, the sweeter the finished Champagne will be. The vast majority of Champagne only has a small amount of sugar added, and is sold as 'Brut' (usually translated as 'very dry'). Very sweet Champagnes were popular in the last century, but nowadays the only sweetish style you may come across is 'Demi-sec'.

The 'pupitres' allegedly derived from the widow Clicquot's kitchen table, used for remuage

With the bottles topped up, the corks can be driven in. These are then wired down to prevent them shooting out. Traditionally the bottles are left to rest for a short while to recover from the trauma of disgorging. They can then be washed, labelled and shipped.

Most Champagne is drunk soon after shipping.

However, it is worth bearing in mind that a good non-vintage Champagne can easily keep for a couple of years. A top vintage Champagne can keep for much longer, sometimes well over ten years. Some of the fresh yeastiness is lost, but the bouquet becomes more mellow and vegetal.

Champagne bottle sizes

Champagne is famous for often coming in large format bottles. The family, with their peculiar names, is as follows:

Name	Equivalent in bottles	Litres
Quarter	¼	0.2
Half	½	0.375
Bottle	1	0.75
Magnum	2	1.5
Jereboam	4	3
Rehoboam	6	4.5
Methuselah	8	6
Salmanazar	12	9
Balthazar	16	12
Nebuchadnezzar	20	15

How to drink Champagne

Quickly, through a straw is my preferred technique; however, for the more conventional among you, Champagne should be served well chilled, and is best appreciated in tall flute glasses. These allow long streamers of bubbles to develop, and like any good wine glass, concentrate the bouquet at the top of the glass. The tasting procedure is the same as for a still wine, with the addition of a comment on the sparkle or 'mousse'. A good Champagne should have plenty of fizz, with persistent streams of fine bubbles running up the glass.

WINE TASTING NOTES

CHAMPAGNE, NON-VINTAGE

Floyd "Cheap champagne or bad sparkling wine is the curse of all weddings, christenings and celebrations. Despite Champagne's exalted position in celebratory culture, it can often be absolutely dreadful. I tasted most of the non-vintage Champagnes which are available and for me the clear leader was Joseph Perrier from Châlons-en-Champagne. It had very fine bubbles and a soft but clean taste, and did not give me heartburn or indigestion. If you really want to splash out, try the Cuvée Josephine in magnum. Hand-corked and therefore treated more lovingly than machine-filled bottles. Quite brilliant. I don't think champagne goes particulary well with food – snacks and canapés, perhaps."

Pedley "Very fine persistent mousse. Palish copper straw. Soft, broad bouquet. Distinctive bready, yeasty character. Some underlying raspberry and beetroot fruit. Just off-dry. High acidity. Moderate alcohol. Mid weight, but with a tight structure. Decent length."

CHAMPAGNE, VINTAGE

Pedley "Excellent mousse. Very fine bubbles. Full straw colour, with just a hint of bronze. Intense, weighty, mature, beetroot and yeast bouquet. Very complex, with a real solidity of fruit, doughiness and bottle development. Dry, mid-high acidity, moderate alcohol. Quite big in the mouth. Almost savoury. Excellent balance and elegance. Long finish."

CHAMPAGNE, VINTAGE ROSE

Pedley "Very good mousse with fine bubbles. Mid intense orangey copper colour. Soft, broad, rich toasty nose. Strawberries and cream. Still showing quite a lot of yeastiness. Very mellow. Dry, mid-high acidity, moderate alcohol. Full and round on the palate. Elegant and long on the finish."

COTEAUX CHAMPENOIS

Pedley "Mid-depth pinkish ruby body. Broad pink rim. High-toned redcurrant and cherry aroma. Just a hint of oak. Almost floral, violet scent. Dry, high acidity, moderate alcohol. A touch of dry tannin. Light bodied, with a little oak showing through. Dry and minerally on the finish. (This wine was a big hit with KF when tasted at the cellars of Joseph Perrier.)"

Floyd food notes

Champagne is the only important wine growing region of France which has not produced from its own soil a traditional cuisine to accompany the wine. The result of this is that the Champenois are gastronomic jackdaws who raid the larders and kitchens of the rest of France: cabbage, partridge and bacon might be stewed in Champagne – a sort of refined Alsace *choucroute,* while the *andouillettes* of Provence might find themselves on the same menu as a cheese fondue from the Savoie. Or you might come across a *matelote* or *bouillabaisse* of freshwater fish, or fine *haute cuisine* such as tender dove breasts stuffed with foie gras or truffles baked in the lightest of pastries. Aware of this freedom of culinary piracy, I have created these two dishes which, like the best of the wine of Champagne, are light, refined, exotic and summery.

Should you be visiting Epernay, you might like to stay in the Hotel Les Berceaux, where they do a wonderful *Croustillant de cochon de lait* (which is, of course, milk-fed suckling pig); or just a few kilometres away, at the Royal Champagne restaurant in Champillon, you will find an excellent *Poulet de Bresse en croute de sel* (Bresse chicken cooked in a salt crust); or at Vinay, at the l'Hostellerie La Briqueterie, you might enjoy brilliant turbot in Champagne sauce (*Blanc de turbot au sauce Champagne*) or fillet of beef cooked in Bouzy, the original red wine of Champagne.

For those who have a few quid to spare, vintage Champagne will accompany the duck and the crayfish splendidly. But both my dishes go well with the red wine of the region, perhaps the Bouzy Rouge from André Clouet, or a wine made by my friends at Joseph Perrier, Coteaux Champenois Cumières Rouge.

P.S. A lot of restaurants in the region offer salmon in Champagne sauce. Salmon and French cooking in my view don't go together, so don't bother. There are more appropriate fish in France. I am afraid I xenophobically regard salmon as the preserve of the Scots, English and Irish.

Ecrevisses au Champagne

(Crayfish in a Champagne sauce)

2 kg/4 lb 8 oz live fresh-water
crayfish, or Dublin Bay
prawns (shell-on, if frozen)

olive oil and butter for frying

4 garlic cloves, finely
chopped

5 shallots, finely chopped

a glass of marc de
Champagne (aromatic spirit
produced from the residue
of Champagne grape
pressing)

250 ml/9 fl oz fish stock

1 bottle of Brut Champagne

300 ml/½ pint double cream

2 or 3 black truffles, finely
sliced

a big pinch of saffron
stamens

a knob of butter

a handful of finely chopped
parsley

salt and pepper

Serves 4 as a main course, 8 as a starter

Fresh truffles are vastly superior to preserved, but if you can't get them, canned or bottled will do; add the juices to the stock.

Wash the crayfish. It's as well to de-vein them before cooking, particularly if you're not sure of the source. To do this, grasp the central tail piece and pull with a twisting motion. Give them another rinse after gutting, and set aside.

Heat the butter and olive oil in a large sauté pan, add the garlic and shallots and cook until soft. Now add the *écrevisses* or prawns, turning them in the pan until they start to turn red, then add the Marc and flame. Add the fish stock and Champagne, bring to the boil and simmer for 2 or 3 minutes until the crayfish or prawns are completely red, then remove them and keep them warm while finishing the sauce.

Over a high heat, reduce the liquid in the pan by half, then lower the heat and whisk in the cream, the sliced truffles, saffron stamens and salt and pepper. Finally work in the knob of butter to produce a smooth, thin, custard-like sauce. Return the *écrevisses* to the sauce to warm through, sprinkle with parsley and serve.

Recommended wine – Champagne

Canard aux petits pois et au Champagne

(Duck with green peas and Champagne)

I free-range, corn-fed duck cut into 4 pieces

a little flour

butter and olive oil for frying

8 large spring onions with some green attached, or eight shallots, peeled

I bulb of garlic, separated into peeled cloves

150 g/5½ oz thick-cut smoked bacon, diced

I bottle of Brut Champagne

a couple of sprigs fresh thyme and a bayleaf

8 small, peeled turnips

4 small, tender leeks cut into 6cm/2½ inch batons

I kg/2 lb 4 oz fresh, shelled peas

half a cos-type lettuce, coarsely chopped

salt and pepper

Recommended wine – Champagne

Serves 4

Dredge the duck pieces in flour. In a large sauté pan fry the duck in a mixture of oil and butter until golden and crispy. Add the onions, the garlic and the smoked bacon pieces and sauté until lightly coloured.

Next add the Champagne, thyme and bayleaf, bring to the boil and cook, uncovered, for half an hour. Then add the turnips and the leeks and cook for twenty minutes or so, until the duck is almost done. Finally add the peas and the lettuce and cook for a further twenty minutes. The sauce will be pale, and slightly thickened. Season to taste with salt and pepper.

APPENDIX

Reading order for technical information

FURTHER READING

Jefford, Andrew (Eng. Lang. Editor). *Larousse Wines and Vineyards of France*, Ebury Press

Johnson, Hugh. *The World Atlas of Wine*, Mitchell Beazley

Robinson, Jancis (Editor). *The Oxford Companion to Wine*, Oxford University Press

Robinson, Jancis. *Vines, Grapes and Wines*, Mitchell Beazley

Stevenson, Tom. *The New Sotheby's Wine Encyclopedia*, Dorling Kindersley

Decanter and *Wine* magazines are also good sources of up-to-date information.

INDEX

Page numbers in *italics* indicate wine tasting notes. Wines and regions using a particular grape are listed under the variety name. All recipes are listed under 'recipe'.

INDEX